Investigations, Tasks, and Rubrics to Teach and Assess Math

Grades 1–6

Pat Lilburn
Alex Ciurak

Math Solutions
Sausalito, California, USA

Math Solutions
One Harbor Drive, Suite 101
Sausalito, CA 94965
www.mathsolutions.com

Library of Congress Cataloging-in-Publication Data
CIP is on file with the Library of Congress.
ISBN 978-1-935099-14-7

Editor: Jamie Ann Cross

Production: Melissa L. Inglis-Elliott

Cover design: Susan Barclay/Barclay Design

Composition: Aptara

Cover photo: Lee Ann Davidson's fifth grade class at South Shades Crest Elementary School, Hoover, Alabama. Videographer: Friday's Films, www.fridaysfilms.com.

Printed in the United States of America on acid-free paper
15 14 13 12   ML   2 3 4 5

A Message from Math Solutions

We at Math Solutions believe that teaching math well calls for increasing our understanding of the math we teach, seeking deeper insights into how students learn mathematics, and refining our lessons to best promote students' learning.

Math Solutions shares classroom-tested lessons and teaching expertise from our faculty of professional development consultants as well as from other respected math educators. Our publications are part of the nationwide effort we've made since 1984 that now includes

- more than five hundred face-to-face professional development programs each year for teachers and administrators in districts across the country;
- professional development books that span all math topics taught in kindergarten through high school;
- videos for teachers and for parents that show math lessons taught in actual classrooms;
- on-site visits to schools to help refine teaching strategies and assess student learning; and
- free online support, including grade-level lessons, book reviews, inservice information, and district feedback, all in our Math Solutions Online Newsletter.

For information about all of the products and services we have available, please visit our website at www.mathsolutions.com. You can also contact us to discuss math professional development needs by calling (800) 868-9092 or by sending an email to *info@mathsolutions.com.*

We're always eager for your feedback and interested in learning about your particular needs. We look forward to hearing from you.

Math Solutions.
FOUNDED BY MARILYN BURNS

SCHOLASTIC

Contents

How to Use This Resource

This resource gives teachers a wide variety of engaging open-ended problem solving tasks and investigations spanning grade levels 1 through 6. Having access to all these grade spans provides opportunities for differentiated problem solving experiences as well as giving teachers a menu of rich mathematical experiences for all students in these grade levels.

The tasks are grouped by content strands that reflect the NCTM Standards as well as the NCTM Curriculum Focal Points. The investigations address more than one content strand and are true problem solving applications of mathematical skills, procedures, and reasoning.

The tasks can generally be completed within a short period of time while the investigations are designed to be developed over a longer time period.

What is an investigative approach to learning math?

An investigative approach to learning math engages students in open-ended tasks and investigations that:

- encourage students to think, question, analyze, criticize, and to solve unfamiliar problems; and
- ask for more than recall of facts or the replication of processes thereby promoting a higher level of thinking.

This approach involves:

- adopting a learner-centred approach to learning and teaching;
- establishing clear expectations of students' demonstrations as a basis for monitoring the progress of student learning; and
- assisting students to work towards demonstrating their learning.

The tasks and investigations include:

Specific strategies

Draw diagrams and tables.
Work systematically.
Recall basic number facts.
Look for patterns.
Make and test predictions.
Generalize.
Look for proof.
List all possibilities.
Use trial and error.
Work backwards.
Estimate.
Collect and organize data.
Identify relevant information.

General behaviors

Discuss.
Work cooperatively.
Work independently.
Communicate using math.
Formulate key questions.
Experiment.
Identify and apply appropriate processes.
Comprehend and explain problems.
Transfer skills.
Check the reasonableness of results.
Self-correct.
Reflect.
Use resources and materials appropriately.
Persevere with problems.

When using an investigative approach, teachers support students by:

- guiding mathematical discussions;
- providing opportunities for students to develop the knowledge, procedures and strategies required for mathematical investigations;
- presenting challenges that require students to pose and solve problems; and
- providing opportunities to reflect on new learning.

Why use mathematical tasks and investigations?

Mathematical tasks and investigations link the learning of mathematical concepts to a real-world context by:

- posing problems to be solved;
- asking questions to be answered;
- describing tasks or challenges to be completed;
- defining issues to be explored in real-life or life-like contexts; and
- providing opportunities for students to use multiple pathways.

Both tasks and investigations require students to:

- identify the math required to undertake the task or investigation;
- describe what they have to do; and
- explain or justify what they have learned.

Open-ended tasks

Open-ended tasks are generally short tasks that:

- have several acceptable responses;
- provide opportunities for students to use multiple pathways to solution;
- require students to use higher order thinking skills beyond the recall of facts;
- allow teachers to observe and learn about each student; and
- can be completed within one session.

Open-ended investigations

Open-ended investigations are longer activities that generally extend over two or three sessions and require students to:

- collect relevant information;
- develop a suitable plan or strategy;
- carry out the plan and revise it when necessary; and
- summarize their results.

The importance of questioning

Questioning of students is an essential tool in the learning process. It not only helps to keep students on track but also helps them clarify and refine concepts, strategies and procedures. While students are involved in tasks and investigations, teachers may find the following discussion starters and questions useful.

Roving conference questions

Tell me about. . . .

How is this different/the same?

Do you remember how we . . .?

What will you try now?

How do you know?

What are you thinking?

Reflection questions

When have you used this before?

What did you discover in math today?

What was something that was new for you?

How did you work it out?

What would you do differently next time?

What were you really happy with? Why?

Assessment Using Rubrics

Assessment Using Rubrics

What are rubrics?

A rubric is an assessment tool that lists the criteria for a piece of work. It lists the things that students, either as individuals or groups, must do or include to receive a certain rating.

Why use rubrics?

Reasons include:

- When students know how their work will be evaluated and what is expected they can improve the quality of their work and revise it before handing it in.
- Assessment is more consistent when everyone knows what is expected for each category.
- Teachers have to clarify what is important or 'what counts' for a particular task.
- Rubrics provide teachers with useful feedback that assists them to plan future teaching.
- Rubrics provide students with useful feedback about their strengths and the areas that need improvement.

How do I use the rubrics in this resource?

The nine rubrics that appear on the following pages were developed using real classrooms and real student samples. The authors know the rubrics work and that students of that age respond as shown in the given criteria and as supported by the authentic student work samples.

From the nine available rubrics, choose a task that is appropriate for your students and decide if you want them to complete the task individually or in small groups.

It is strongly recommended that you discuss with and/or give students the rubric that accompanies a task before they do the task. Students then understand what is expected and how they will be evaluated and can judge and revise their work before they hand in the task.

Sometimes you will find that completed work contains criteria that do not exactly match a category. The work may contain elements that fit into two categories or elements that are not included on the rubric. In such cases, you will need to use your knowledge of the student's previous performance and work to decide how to categorize it.

How do I design my own rubric?

When you give students a task from this book (other than the ones that have an accompanying rubric) and you wish to make your own rubric, there are two ways you can do this, described below.

Method 1

1. Choose a suitable task and, after an initial class discussion to ensure all students understand it, ask them to do the task individually.

2. Collect students' responses and use them to work out categories and the criteria that put students' responses into those categories. You can do this yourself or you can ask the students to say what things they consider to be important in each category.

3. Don't tell students what category you determined their response to be in, but do make it clear to students what criteria their work needs to show in order to be assessed in each category. You either can do this through discussion or by sharing a copy of the rubric that shows the criteria for each category.

4. Alter the initial task slightly and ask students to do it again, but this time with knowledge of what they need to do to be assessed in each category. For example, an initial task may have been: *One-fourth of a bunch of flowers are pink. What might the bunch of flowers look like?* The new task could be: *One-third of the fruit in a bowl are apples. What might the bowl of fruit look like?*

5. Assess this second piece of work according to the criteria that you have decided for each category.

Method 2

1. Choose a suitable task.

2. Work out appropriate categories and criteria for the task without student input.

3. Tell students what criteria they will have to display to have their work evaluated in each particular category and provide time for them to work on the chosen task.

4. Collect students' work and assess it according to the criteria that you have decided for each category.

Reproducible Rubric Templates

Rubric templates that you may find useful when designing your own rubrics have also been included at the back of this book (pages 134 to 136).

Nine Assessment Rubrics

Assessment Rubric 1

This task was given to grades 1 and 2 students. Relevant work samples are shown for each category.

> **Task:** *There are seven shirts hanging on a clothes line. Some are white and some are blue. There are no other colors. How many of each color might there be?*

Category	Criteria
Beyond expectations ⟶	Student draws, or uses numbers to describe, all possible combinations of shirts. That is: 1 + 6, 2 + 5, 3 + 4, 4 + 3, 5 + 2, and 6 + 1. (Note: 7 + 0 or 0 + 7 does not apply since the task states there are some of each color.)
Accomplishes task: central mathematical idea is understood ⟶	Student draws or writes one or more, but not all, possible combinations of shirts. The examples given are correct.
Makes some progress at task but not completed satisfactorily ⟶	Student does one of the following: a) Draws more than one line of shirts but at least one line is incorrect. b) Draws seven shirts but all seven are the same color. (See student work sample.)
Little or no understanding evident ⟶	Student does one of the following: a) Makes an incorrect attempt by drawing the wrong number of shirts. b) Makes no attempt.

Student Work Samples

Beyond expectations
Student draws and writes all possible combinations.

1 + 6 = 7

3 + 4 = 7

2 + 5 = 7

4 + 3 = 7

5 + 2 = 7

6 + 1 = 7

Accomplishes task
Student draws one combination only.

Makes some progress
Student draws all shirts one color.

Little or no understanding
Student draws six shirts.

Assessment Rubric 2

This task was given to grades 1 and 2 students. Relevant work samples are shown for each category.

Task: *One-half of a flag is one color and the other half is another color. Draw what the flag might look like.*

Category	Criteria
Beyond expectations	Student draws more than one correct flag. All flags drawn clearly show equal parts. In one or more of the flags there is evidence of understanding equivalence (for example, that one-half is equal to two-fourths, three-sixths, and so on).
Accomplishes task: understands central mathematical idea	Student draws more than one flag and all are correct. In the flags drawn, one-half is shown as two equal parts and this is demonstrated with flags that are divided into two equal parts in more than one way.
Completes task but shows only limited understanding	Student's completed work shows one of the following: a) Only one flag drawn and it is correct. b) More than one flag drawn but all have been divided into two equal parts in the same way. (Accept flags with two parts that are not equal but are close to equal.) (See student work sample.)
Makes some progress but shows misconceptions in key concepts	Student shows two or more obviously unequal parts in one or more of the flags drawn.
Little or no understanding evident	Student does one of the following: a) Makes no attempt. b) Makes some attempts, none of which are correct.

Student Work Samples

Beyond expectations
Student demonstrates an understanding that one-half is the same as two-fourths.

 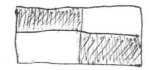

Accomplishes task
Student represents one-half in more than one way.

Completes task but shows only limited understanding
Student divides all flags into halves in the same way.

Makes some progress
Student represents flags in unequal parts.

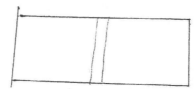

Little or no understanding
Student represents one-half in none of the flags.

Assessment Rubric 3

This task was given to grades 1 and 2 students. Relevant work samples are shown for each category.

Task: *I am thinking of a number between ten and one hundred. Its tens digit is two fewer than its units digit. What might the number be? Write all possible numbers.*

Category	Criteria
Task fully accomplished →	Student writes all possible numbers. There are seven: 13, 24, 35, 46, 57, 68, and 79. Student may state how he or she knows he or she has found all numbers.
Task partly accomplished but central mathematical idea is understood →	Student writes one or more correct numbers and no incorrect numbers. (You may accept one number in a group that is written, for example, as 60/8 rather than 68 since the student still shows an understanding of place value.) (See student work sample.)
Shows some understanding but has misconceptions →	Student writes more correct than incorrect numbers. Do not accept reversals as correct numbers, for example, 42 instead of 24.
Very limited understanding →	Student writes more incorrect than correct numbers or the same number of each, but must have at least one correct number. Allow reversals for this group (for example, 53 is a reversal so it is allowed in this category).
No understanding evident →	Student does one of the following: a) Makes no attempt. b) Writes numbers that are all incorrect (not reversals).

Student Work Samples

Task fully accomplished
Student represents all possible numbers.

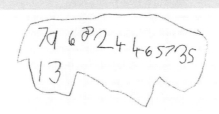

Task party accomplished
Student represents no incorrect numbers; 60/8 accepted as correct.

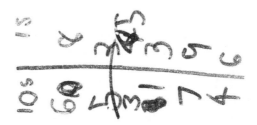

Shows some understanding but has misconceptions
Student represents more numbers correctly than incorrectly.

Very limited understanding
Student represents more numbers incorrectly than correctly.

71   32   53

No understanding
Student incorrectly represents all numbers.

45   54
  67 76   92

Assessment Rubric 4

This task was given to grades 3 and 4 students. Relevant work samples are shown for each category.

Task: *One-fourth of a bunch of balloons is red. Draw what the bunch of balloons might look like.*

Category		Criteria
Beyond expectations	→	Student draws *more than one* correct bunch of balloons and each bunch represents a different equivalent fraction. For example: 1 out of 4, 2 out of 8, 3 out of 12 and so on are colored red.
Accomplishes task: clear understanding	→	Student draws *only one* bunch of balloons and that bunch correctly shows a fraction that is equivalent to $\frac{1}{4}$ but not 1 out of 4. For example: 5 out of 20, 2 out of 8, 4 out of 16.
Accomplishes task: limited understanding or misconception	→	Student does one of the following; a) Draws *one* bunch of balloons that shows 1 out of 4 balloons colored red. b) Draws *more than one* bunch of balloons with some correct but at least one incorrect. (See student work sample.)
Little or no understanding evident	→	Student does one of the following: a) Makes no attempt. b) Makes an attempt, none of which are correct.

Student Work Samples

Beyond expectations
Student draws three bunches of balloons, each showing a different equivalent fraction.

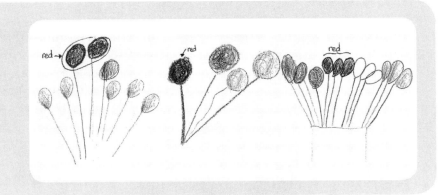

Accomplishes task: clear understanding
Student draws one bunch of balloons showing $\frac{2}{8}$.

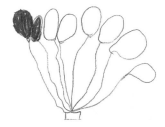

Accomplishes task: limited understanding
Student represents two drawings correctly and one incorrectly.

Little or no understanding
Student draws six red balloons.

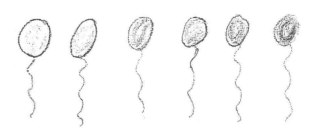

Assessment Rubric 5

This task was given to grades 3 and 4 students. Relevant work samples are shown for each category.

> **Task:** *The digits in a three-digit number between three hundred and five hundred add up to nine. What might the number be? Write all possible numbers.*

Category	Criteria
Task fully accomplished	Student writes all possible numbers and no other numbers. There are thirteen: 306, 315, 324, 333, 342, 351, 360, 405, 414, 423, 432, 441, and 450. Student may state how he or she knows they have found all numbers.
Task partly accomplished	Student does one of the following: a) Writes one or more but not all of the possible numbers and no incorrect numbers. b) Writes all possible numbers and then repeats some of them.
Makes some progress at task but not completed satisfactorily	Student writes more numbers correctly than incorrectly. This includes students who write all possible numbers but also include incorrect numbers. (Numbers can be incorrect because their digits do not add to nine or because the numbers are not between three hundred and five hundred.)
Minimal progress made: lacks understanding	Student writes more incorrect than correct numbers. To be included in this category, students must have at least one-third of their numbers correct.
Little or no understanding evident	Student's completed work shows one of the following: a) No attempt has been made. b) Fewer than one-third of the numbers written are correct.

Student Work Samples

306   405
315   414
324   423
333   432
342   441
351

360   450

Task fully accomplished
Student represents all possible numbers.

Task partly accomplished
Student represents all numbers and repeats some numbers.

Sample A:

333 450 432
315 405 441
351 324 414
306 342 432
360 423 423

Sample B:
Student represents some correct numbers and no incorrect ones.

333 423 441

Makes some progress
Student represents more numbers correctly than incorrectly.

Sample A:

450 414
333 306
360 441
405 431
315 314

Sample B:

333
405
603
414

Minimal progress made
Student correctly represents four out of ten numbers.

333 243 432 225
207 225 360 260
441 319

Little or no understanding
Student correctly represents one out of eight numbers only.

300 ⟵⟶ 500
306   402
309   406
399   409

Assessment Rubric 6

This task was given to grades 3 and 4 students. Relevant work samples are shown for each category.

Task: *The number 17 cannot be divided equally by either 2 or 3. What other numbers are not divisible by either 2 or 3?*

Category	Criteria
Beyond expectations	Student's work displays *all* of the following: a) at least twenty numbers are written *and* b) all numbers written are correct *and* c) some or all of the numbers written extend beyond one hundred.
Task accomplished: central mathematical idea is understood	Student writes at least five numbers all of which are correct and some or all of the numbers extend beyond twenty. (In this category, you might also include students who satisfy all the criteria of the first category but who incorrectly represent only one number.)
Task accomplished: limited understanding	Student does one of the following: a) Writes numbers that do not extend beyond twenty but that are correct. (See student work sample B.) b) Writes fewer than five numbers but all are correct. c) Writes numbers more and fewer than fifty where all numbers fewer than fifty are correct, even if some or all of those more than fifty are not. (See student work sample A.)
Minimal progress made	If a student's work does not qualify for any of the above categories but if more than 50 percent of the numbers written are correct, then their work is in this category.
No understanding evident	Student's completed work shows one of the following: a) No attempt has been made. b) It is obvious that the task is not understood. c) More than 50 percent of the numbers written are not correct. (Other than where student's work fits the third category.)

Student Work Samples

Beyond expectations
Student correctly represents all numbers and extends some beyond one hundred.

1,5,7,11,13,17,19,23,25,29,31,35,37,
41,43,47,49,53,55,59,61,65,
67,71,73,77,79,83,85,89,91,95,
97,101,103,107,109,113,115,119,121,125,
27,131,133,137,139,143,145,149,151,155,

Task accomplished: central idea understood
Student represents at least five numbers, some above twenty.

11,13,7,19,5,
23,29

Task accomplished: limited understanding
Student correctly represents all numbers fewer than 50

Sample A:

17 5 7 1 19 23
11 13 41 25

573

Sample B:
Student represents numbers that do not extend beyond twenty but are correct. ↓

11,19,13,5,7

Minimal progress made
Student correctly represents more than 50 percent of numbers, although 27, 33, and 51 are incorrect.

13 7 23 11 27 33 37 41 19 51

No understanding
Student does not understand task.

1 r1   2 r6   0 3r1
3) 4   7) 20   7) 22

2 r2   0 5r2   0 r5
4) 10   4) 22   6) 11

Assessment Rubric 7

This task was given to grades 5 and 6 students. Relevant work samples are shown for each category.

Task: *Draw various number lines that each have at least six numbers marked at equal intervals and include the number 180,000.*

Category	Criteria
Above expectations ⟶	Student completes two or more number lines either correctly or with minor errors. Examples of minor errors include: • writing fewer than six numbers on their line • missing a zero within or on the end of a number (See student work sample.) • adding a zero or zeroes to a number
Demonstrates clear understanding ⟶	Student completes at least one number line either correctly or with what you consider to be a minor error. In this category, you might include students with a number interval error who have clearly shown strong counting ability in other sections of their number lines.
Demonstrates some understanding ⟶	Student completes at least one number line but in the lines completed has more than one minor error and/or a major error. Examples of major errors include: • a number interval error • interval spacing absent or very irregular • correct numbers written but in descending order (Number lines can go in both directions from zero but positive numbers ascend to the right.) • numbers written are in ten thousands instead of hundred thousands • the numbers are written between the interval lines rather than above
Not satisfactory ⟶	Student attempts or completes at least one number line but has more than one major error.
No understanding evident ⟶	Student does one of the following: a) Makes no attempt. b) Draws a line but does not write numbers. c) Draws a number line with numbers that are totally incorrect.

Student Work Samples

Above expectations

Student misses a zero with the number 200,000. (Shown here is one of two number lines drawn by student.)

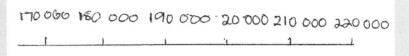

Demonstrates clear understanding

Student demonstrates strong counting ability but makes an error in the last number.

Demonstrates some understanding

Student representation of interval spacing is absent and irregular.

Not satisfactory

Student represents numbers written between interval lines and incorrectly represents numbers by using a decimal point.

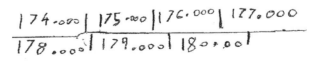

No understanding

Student incorrectly represents numbers.

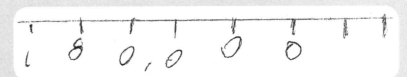

Assessment Rubric 8

This task was given to grades 5 and 6 students. Relevant work samples are shown for each category.

> **Task:** *Finn wrote some equations that had an answer of 20. He only used one subtraction sign, one division sign, and one set of parentheses in each equation. What might his equations look like?*

Category   Criteria

Beyond expectations ⟶ All the equations that are written are correct. Student demonstrates both of the following equation types:

     1. $(60 − 20) ÷ 2 = 20$

     2. $100 ÷ (6 − 1) = 20$

Student may also state that the parentheses must be around the subtraction as, according to convention, division is done before subtraction. For this reason, equations of the type $(42 ÷ 2) − 1 = 20$ or $30 − (40 ÷ 4) = 20$ are not acceptable.

Demonstrates clear understanding ⟶ Student writes more than one equation and all are correct but of only one type. Include in this category any students who have written at least three correct equations but who have made a minor arithmetical error in other equations (for example, subtracting incorrectly.) (An arithmetical error does not include using parentheses around division or making an error with the order of operations.)

Demonstrates limited understanding of key ideas ⟶ Student does one of the following:

a) Writes one equation only and it is correct.

b) Writes more than one equation and approximately half of them are correct. (See student work sample.)

Shows misconceptions in key ideas ⟶ Student's completed work shows one of the following:

a) Fewer than half the equations are correct.

b) No equations are correct because they have one or more of these errors:
- signs and operations other than those specified are used
- parentheses are used around division unnecessarily
- the order of operations is incorrect
- the equations have arithmetical errors

No progress ⟶ Student makes no attempt.

Student Work Samples

Beyond expectations
Student represents both equation types.

$80 \div (28 - 24) = 20$ $(124 - 24) \div 5 = 20$
$80 \div (27 - 23) = 20$ $(123 - 23) \div 5 = 20$
$80 \div (26 - 22) = 20$ $(122 - 22) \div 5 = 20$
$80 \div (25 - 21) = 20$ $(121 - 21) \div 5 = 20$
$80 \div (24 - 20) = 20$ $(120 - 20) \div 5 = 20$

Demonstrates clear understanding
Student represents correct equations but only one type.

$(27 - 7) \div 1 = 20$

$(30 - 10) \div 1 = 20$

Demonstrates limited understanding
Student correctly represents half of the equations.

$21 + (1 \div 1) = 20$
$(185 - 43) \div 7 = 20$
$\;\;\;\;\; 55 - (70 \div) = 20$
$(41 - 1) \div 2 = 20$

Shows misconceptions

Student's work shows an arithmetic error.

⟶ $(40 - 10) \div 2 = 20$

Student's work shows use of operations other than those specified.

⟶ $(4 + 2 \times 3) \div 5 \times 10 = 20$

Student's work shows an incorrect order and unnecessary use of parentheses.

⟶ $1 - (42 \div 2) = 20$

Assessment Rubric 9

This task was given to grades 5 and 6 students. Relevant work samples are shown for each category.

Task: *Sharmin wrote fractions that were smaller than $\frac{1}{4}$. What fractions might she have written?*

Category	Criteria
Beyond expectations →	Student writes one or more unit fractions (common fractions with one as the numerator) and one or more common fractions with numerators other than one. All fractions written are correct.
	Student may give some examples and then make general statements about possible fractions rather than writing lists of them.
	Student may also write decimals and/or percentages as well as common fractions and these must be correct.
Accomplishes task satisfactorily →	Student only writes unit fractions. (Not any with a numerator other than one.) All those written are correct.
	Student may also write decimals and/or percentages and they must be correct.
Task partly accomplished but some misconceptions →	Student writes unit and/or non-unit fractions but has one or more errors. To be included in this category, student must have no more than 25 percent incorrect. Errors may include:
	• incorrect fractions (See student work sample A.)
	• fractions written incorrectly (for example, $\frac{0.3}{4}$) (See student work sample B.)
	• a general statement that is incorrect or that does not apply to all situations
Limited understanding →	Student writes one or more fractions but more than 25 percent are incorrect.
No understanding evident →	Student's completed work shows one of the following: a) No attempt has been made. b) All the fractions written are incorrect.

Student Work Samples

Beyond expectations
Student represents unit fractions and fractions with numerators other than one.

$\frac{1}{5}$ $\frac{1}{6}$ $\frac{1}{7}$ $\frac{1}{8}$ $\frac{1}{9}$ $\frac{1}{10}$

$\frac{2}{10}$ $\frac{2}{12}$ $\frac{2}{14}$ $\frac{2}{16}$ $\frac{2}{18}$ $\frac{2}{20}$

$\frac{3}{15}$ $\frac{3}{18}$ $\frac{3}{21}$ $\frac{3}{24}$ $\frac{3}{27}$ $\frac{3}{30}$

$\frac{4}{20}$ $\frac{4}{24}$ $\frac{4}{28}$ $\frac{4}{32}$ $\frac{4}{36}$ $\frac{4}{40}$

$\frac{5}{25}$ $\frac{5}{30}$ $\frac{5}{35}$ $\frac{5}{40}$ $\frac{5}{45}$ $\frac{5}{50}$

Accomplishes task satisfactorily
Student represents only unit fractions.

$\frac{1}{4}$ $\frac{1}{5}$ $\frac{1}{6}$ $\frac{1}{7}$ $\frac{1}{8}$ $\frac{1}{9}$ $\frac{1}{10}$

$\frac{1}{11}$ $\frac{1}{12}$ $\frac{1}{13}$ $\frac{1}{14}$ $\frac{1}{15}$ $\frac{1}{16}$ $\frac{1}{17}$

$\frac{1}{18}$ $\frac{1}{19}$ $\frac{1}{20}$ $\frac{1}{21}$ $\frac{1}{22}$ $\frac{1}{23}$

Task partly accomplished
Student's work shows incorrect fractions.
$\frac{1}{3}$ is larger than $\frac{1}{4}$. →

Sample A:

$\frac{1}{3}$ $\frac{7}{56}$ $\frac{7}{55}$

$\frac{7}{54}$

$\frac{1}{8}$ $\frac{9}{72}$

Sample B:
Student's work shows fractions written incorrectly.

↓

$\frac{0.7}{4}$ $\frac{0.8}{4}$ $\frac{0.9}{4}$

Limited understanding
Student incorrectly represents more than 25 percent of fractions.

$\frac{2}{3}$ $\frac{1}{2}$

$\frac{1}{1}$ $\frac{1}{5}$ $\frac{2}{10}$

No understanding
Student incorrectly represents all fractions.

$\frac{2}{4}$ $\frac{1}{2}$ $\frac{1}{4}$ $\frac{3}{1}$

Tasks and Investigations, Grades 1–2

Tasks • Strand: Number

Money

If I have four identical coins in my pocket, how much money might I have?	*Ask students to be systematic and to find out how many different amounts they might have.*
I have two of the same coin and my friend has one coin. We have the same amount of money. How much might we have?	*Note if students develop a system when recording possibilities.*
I have $2 in coins. All my coins are the same. What coins and how many of each might I have?	*Encourage students to list all possibilities.*
A game costs $10 and you pay for it using coins. What coins might you use?	*Allow students to use play money to show the coins they could tender. Share different possibilities.*
In my hand I have a coin that is worth fewer than 50 cents. What coin might I have in my hand?	*Vary this activity, for example: a coin worth more than 20 cents.*
Kayla bought five items at the market. The most expensive was $12.75 and the cheapest was $7.05. What might the price of the other three items be?	*The focus here is on ordering amounts of money.*

Fractions

My friend and I each had a piece of paper the same shape. We each cut our shape in halves but when I looked I saw that my halves were a different shape than my friend's halves. What might our original pieces of paper have looked like?	*Squares and rectangles can be halved in different ways and are the obvious choice here, but shapes with curved edges, such as ovals, can also be halved in different ways. Encourage students to think about irregular as well as regular shapes.*
One half of a flag is one color and the other half is another color. Draw what the flag might look like.	*Note if the flag design is simple or complex. Which students show an understanding of equivalence by coloring their flag creatively?*

See Rubric 2, page 8.

Tasks • Strand: Number

Decimals and Percentages

For this topic there are only tasks for grades 3–6, as students only need experience decimals in an informal way before these years.

Numeration

A three-digit number contains two 5s. What are the possible numbers?	*Make sure students understand that they have to write numbers with three digits. At this level students will probably not be systematic in their recording. You might like to do this as a class activity after students have had a go by themselves.*
Find items in the classroom that are in groups. Make a number label to show how many things there are in each group.	*Students could draw their groups on sheets of paper and write the number of items per group beside each drawing. Share completed drawings.*
Write a list of things in your classroom that you could count by twos, fives, or tens.	*This task could be done in three different sessions, one session for each counting number. Students could work in small groups and then share their findings with the class.*
List things you know that come in groups larger than twenty.	*Like the previous task, students could work in small groups and then share their responses with the class.*
Tim wrote a two-digit number that had the same number in its tens place as in its units place. What number might Tim have written?	*Make sure students understand what two-digit means. Which students can list possible numbers systematically and know that they have listed all numbers?*
When Issy was counting out loud from zero to one hundred by a number other than one, one of the numbers she said was "sixty-three." What number might she have been counting by?	*Possible numbers are three, seven, nine, and twenty-one. Allow students to use a calculator or ruler if they want.*

Tasks • Strand: Number

I am thinking of a number between ten and one hundred. Its tens digit is two fewer than its units digit. What might the number be? Write all possible numbers.	*Note the students who do this systematically. Also note those students who do not understand the language of place value.* See Rubric 3, page 10.
If you start at twenty, and count by twos, you land on fifty. Starting at twenty, what other numbers can you count by and still land on fifty?	*Possible numbers are three, five, six, ten, fifteen, and thirty. Allow students to use a calculator or ruler if they want.*
When Eric woke up he stood and looked at his surroundings. Later, the only thing he could clearly remember was seeing the number 12. Where might he have been and where might he have seen the number 12?	*Can students recognize numbers in everyday life? Are they aware that numbers can have different meanings in different situations? Possible scenarios for Eric include: seeing the number 12 on a clock or a mailbox, or seeing a price tag with 12 on it.*
Finn wrote a number. He counted how many straight lines he had used to form the number and found there were two. What number might he have written?	*This depends on the style that students use to write numbers. If numbers are written with the following number of straight lines then numbers 1, 2, and 9 have one straight line, 5 and 7 have two straight lines, 4 has three straight lines, and 3, 6, 8, and 0 have no straight lines. Therefore, numbers below 100 that Finn might have written include 5, 7, 11, 12, 19, 21, 22, 29, 35, 37, 50, 53, 56, 58, 65, 67, 70, 73, 76, 78, 85, 87, 91, 92, and 99.*
I started at ninety-three and counted backwards by 5s. What are some numbers that I might have said?	*Discuss possible numbers. Ask students what the numbers have in common (the numbers end in 8 or 3).*

Tasks • Strand: Number

Operations

The total of two numbers is ten. What might the two numbers be?	*Vary this task by changing the number. Do students know what the term* total *means? Allow students to use counters to help them.*
The total of three numbers is ten. What might the three numbers be?	*This is similar to the previous task. Again, vary it by changing the number.*
Draw a picture where there are two more girls than boys.	*Share the completed pictures so students can see the range of responses.*
There are seven shirts hanging on a clothes line. Some are white and some are blue. There are no other colors. How many of each color might there be?	*Note those students who understand that the total number of shirts is 7. Also note those students who write numbers to represent their drawings.* See Rubric 1, page 6.
There are bats and balls in a sports basket. There are more bats than balls. How many of each item might there be in the basket?	*This task is more open than the previous one because it does not state the total number of bats and balls. Ask some students to say how many more bats than balls they have drawn.*
Sam tossed two six-sided dice and made a total of seven. What number of dots might have been on each dice?	*The purpose of this and the next two tasks is for students to think about the addition process in a different way. Share the range of possible answers.*
Emily tossed three six-sided dice and made a total of twelve. What number of dots might have been on each dice?	*Discuss if 6, 2, and 4 is the same as 4, 6, and 2 or 2, 4, and 6 and so on.*
How many different ways can you get a total of thirteen when you toss three six-sided dice? Record each way.	*This task goes a little further than the previous two by asking students to record all possible answers.*
A collection of eight counters can be put into two groups with the same number in each group (four). What other numbers of counters can be put into two groups so that there is the same number in each group?	*Which students realize that this can be any even number? Provide counters so students can discover this for themselves.*

Tasks • Strand: Number

Using one deck of cards what card combinations make a total of twelve?	*Before asking students to do this activity, explain that an ace has a value of 1 and a picture card has a value of 10. Encourage students to use combinations of two or more cards. For example, 5 and 5 and 2; King and 2; 7 and 4 and an ace.*
I joined two groups together and got an answer of fifteen. How many might have been in each group?	*This task highlights the joining together aspect of addition. Share the range of possible responses.*
I subtracted one number from another and got an answer of nine. What numbers might I have started with?	*Note the methods students use to do this and the size of the numbers that they are confident working with.*

Patterns and Algebra

Ben made a 2, 1, 2, 1 . . . pattern by repeatedly placing two shells and one rock in a row. What 2, 1 patterns can you make with other materials?	*Do students just use other materials or do they use color, shape, and position to form 2, 1 patterns? For example: a 2, 1 color pattern can be formed by repeatedly placing two red cubes and one yellow cube in a row; a 2, 1 shape pattern can be formed from two squares and one circle. The emphasis is on making students aware of the different ways the same number pattern can be represented.*
Jack had some Popsicle sticks and some bottle tops. He made a pattern that used the same number of each object. What might his pattern have looked like?	*Supply suitable objects to students. Ask some students to describe their pattern with numbers.*
Grace made a pattern with three different objects. What might her pattern have looked like?	*This task is similar to the previous two. Provide a range of objects and share the completed patterns. Ask some students to describe their pattern.*

Tasks • Strand: Measurement

Weight

Find items that are heavier than your backpack. Find items that are lighter than your backpack. Find items that weigh about the same as your backpack.	*These tasks focus on the language of weight and comparing by lifting. Allow students to talk about their findings so they practice using the language of weight.*
Find an object that will balance five CDs.	*Students need a pan balance to do this. Can they find different objects?*
Find two objects that together will balance five CDs.	*This is similar to the previous task. Do students realize that the two objects will balance the object in the previous task?*
Find something that is heavier than a tennis ball but lighter than your backpack.	*If the two items mentioned in the activity are not available substitute them for others. Note how students find appropriate items. Do they guess or do they lift the items to check?*
Find two different objects that have a similar weight.	*Note how students do this. Do they compare weights by lifting? Allow students to talk about what they found and how they did this.*

Volume and Capacity

Kate filled a container with two cups of sand. What container might she have filled?	*You will need to provide sand, cups, and a variety of containers. The language that students use while doing such tasks is important so make sure to let them describe what they do and find.*
Show the students a container such as a shoebox. Say, "Find a container that takes up more space than the shoebox and one that takes up less space."	*Note how students choose containers. Do students focus on the space inside the containers or do they only focus on the base or length? What methods do students use to find the amount of space taken up?*
Find some containers that are about half full when a cup of water is poured into them.	*Check that students understand the language of approximation by doing this task and similar ones such as, "When a cup of water is poured into a container, the container is almost full [or empty]. What might the container be?"*

Tasks • Strand: Measurement

Length and Perimeter

Make a paper clip chain. Find things that are the same length, longer, and shorter than your chain. What are some things that your chain will fit around exactly?	*You will need lots of paper clips. While students are comparing their chain to objects, it is important to let them talk about their experience using the language of length.*
Find something that is about half your height.	*Do students only measure vertical objects or do they understand that height is a length measurement? Discuss why found objects vary among students (for example, some students are taller than others).*
Can you find something that is twice as wide as your arm span?	*This is similar to the previous task. Do students understand that width is a length measurement? You could also ask them to find something twice as wide as the doorway.*
What can you find that is the same length as eight Popsicle sticks?	*Note if students place the sticks end to end without gaps.*

Area

What are some things that you can cover with ten tiles exactly?	*Students will need ten tiles to do this task. Check that the tiles are placed together without gaps.*

Time

What is something you could do that takes exactly the same time as it takes sand to run through a timer?	*You will need a sand timer for this task. It is a good idea to let students work in small groups to find things they can do.*
What things take about the same amount of time as writing your name?	*Note how students measure how long it takes to write their name and then use this to find other activities that take about the same time. Discuss if all names take the same time to write and why the time may differ.*

Tasks • Strand: Geometry

Location and Position

Place a circular shape on the floor or draw a circle on the board. Arrange other shapes (or objects) to the left or right of the circle. Ask, "Which shapes are right of the circle? Which shapes are left of the circle?"	*The purpose of this task is to see if students are confident with left and right.*
Draw some things that are behind you. Draw some things that are in front of you.	*This task will show you if students understand the meaning of certain location or position words. Vary the words to suit your purpose.*
Draw a picture that shows a dog inside a kennel, a cat beside the kennel, a bird above the kennel, and a food bowl outside the kennel.	*It is important that students share their pictures so they can see the range of correct responses and realize that different pictures fit the description.*

Two-Dimensional Shape

Draw items in your room that are triangular in shape.	*Do students draw any three-dimensional shapes that have triangular faces? Adapt this task with other shapes.*
Draw a picture that has symmetry.	*Ask various students to say why their picture is symmetrical. Discuss where the line of symmetry is in each picture. You could ask half the students in your class to do this task and the other half to do the next task and then compare the features of the pictures in each group.*
Draw a picture that does not have symmetry.	*As for the above task, ask students to say how they know their picture is not symmetrical. Discuss what students would have to do to make their picture symmetrical.*
I traced around something in the room and it looked like this: ☐ What might I have traced around?	*The purpose of this task is to see if students understand the relationship between two-dimensional shapes and the faces of three-dimensional shapes.*

Tasks • Strand: Geometry

Three-Dimensional Shape

I picked up an object and placed it on a ramp. It slid down the ramp. What object might I have picked up?	*It is a good idea to set up a ramp so students can test their choice of objects.*
Olivia used a piece of modeling clay to make a shape that had only curved surfaces. Her shape was not a ball. What might it have been?	*Students will need modeling material to make their shape. You could also ask students to make a shape that does not have any curves. Ask some students to describe their shape. The emphasis here is on the range of possible shapes and the language, for example, curved, surface, corners, edges.*
Elad picked up an object that had both curved and plane surfaces. What object might he have picked up?	*Which students understand the terms curved and plane? Ask different students to point out the curved surfaces and the plane surfaces on the objects that are found.*

Tasks • Strand: Probability and Data

Probability

A mystery visitor was coming to our class. We made a list of likely visitors. Make a list of likely visitors to your class.	*When you have made your list, you could ask students to put them in order of most likely to least likely.*
I asked Mom a question and she replied, "Impossible." What might the question be?	*It is important to discuss the answers to this. Students need to realize that what is impossible for some will not be so for others.*

Data

Farmer Brown has seventeen animals. He has four different types of animals. Draw a graph to show what they might be.	*Encourage students to be creative. It is important that they have the opportunity to see the variety of graphs that are drawn.*
This graph shows the responses of some students to a question asked by their teacher. What question might the students have been asked? 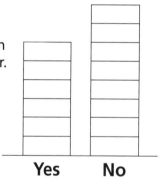	*Discuss the suggested questions and decide as a class if they are reasonable.*
What might this be the graph of?	*Do students make reasonable suggestions? Share the responses so students see that there is a range of possible responses.*

Red	☐ ☐ ☐
Green	☐ ☐ ☐ ☐ ☐ ☐ ☐
Yellow	☐ ☐ ☐ ☐

Investigation 1

Breakfast menu!

How many boxes of cereal would your family eat in one year?

Write or draw what you found below.

Things to consider

How many people in your family eat cereal?

How many bowls of cereal can be filled from a full box of cereal?

How many bowls of cereal does your family eat in one day, one week, one month?

Calculator magic

Aron started with number 10 on his calculator and ended with 20 without clearing the calculator display.

Using a calculator, investigate and record the ways that Aron might have used to get from 10 to 20.

Things to consider

Do you think Aron pressed lots of buttons or not many?

Can you use different operations to get from 10 to 20?

From *Investigations, Tasks, and Rubrics to Teach and Assess Math* by Pat Lilburn and Alex Ciurak. © 2010 by Scholastic Inc. Permission granted to photocopy for nonprofit use in a classroom or similar place dedicated to face-to-face educational instruction.

Investigation 3

Tooth count

How many teeth do you have? Do all children have the same number of teeth?

Use a mirror to help you count your teeth. Draw a tooth map to show the number of top teeth and the number of bottom teeth.

Things to consider

Have you lost any teeth? How will you show this on your tooth map?
How will you find out if all children have the same number of teeth?

Investigation 4

How old?

The ages of the people in my family total 120. In your class, are there more families whose ages total more than 120 than there are families whose ages total fewer than 120?

Record your findings below.

Things to consider

How will you collect the information?

Do you need a calculator to help add the ages?

Do all families have the same number of people?

From *Investigations, Tasks, and Rubrics to Teach and Assess Math* by Pat Lilburn and Alex Ciurak. © 2010 by Scholastic Inc. Permission granted to photocopy for nonprofit use in a classroom or similar place dedicated to face-to-face educational instruction.

Investigation 5

Animal legs

My friend said that most animals have four legs. Do you agree?

Record your findings.

Things to consider

What animals do you know that have four legs?
What animals do you know have a number of legs other than four?

Odd or even?

Do more people in your class have a street address with an odd number than a street address with an even number?

Draw a graph in the space below to show what you find.

Things to consider

How will you collect the information?

How do you know if a number is odd or even?

What type of graph will you draw?

From *Investigations, Tasks, and Rubrics to Teach and Assess Math* by Pat Lilburn and Alex Ciurak. © 2010 by Scholastic Inc. Permission granted to photocopy for nonprofit use in a classroom or similar place dedicated to face-to-face educational instruction.

Investigation 7

Coffee time

Do all the teachers at your school drink more or less than a *bucket* of coffee each week during school hours?

Write or draw what you found.

Things to consider

How will you measure how much coffee teachers drink at school?
Is there a recording sheet you can design that will help you collect information?
How much more or less than a *bucket* of coffee is drunk?

Investigation 8

Finger length

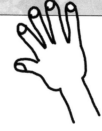

How long are your fingers?

Trace around one of your hands and mark each finger to show the order of length.

Things to consider

How will you measure your fingers?

How will you compare your fingers to find their order from longest to shortest?

Does everyone have fingers in the same order as yours?

Are the matching fingers on each of your hands the same length?

From *Investigations, Tasks, and Rubrics to Teach and Assess Math* by Pat Lilburn and Alex Ciurak. © 2010 by Scholastic Inc. Permission granted to photocopy for nonprofit use in a classroom or similar place dedicated to face-to-face educational instruction.

Investigation **9**

My school

Draw a map in the space below of your school. Make sure to show the areas outside such as parking lots, sidewalks, and playgrounds.

Things to consider

How will you show important features on your map?
What is the largest thing at your school? How will you show that it is the largest?

Investigation 10

Number sort

Daria sorted the numbers 1 to 20 into these two groups:

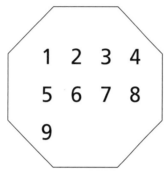

| 1 2 3 4 |
| 5 6 7 8 |
| 9 |

Numbers with one digit

| 10 11 12 13 |
| 14 15 16 17 |
| 18 19 20 |

Numbers with two digits

Investigate other ways to sort the numbers 1 to 20 into groups.

Things to consider

What other ways can you sort the numbers into two groups?
Is it possible to sort the numbers into three or more groups?

From *Investigations, Tasks, and Rubrics to Teach and Assess Math* by Pat Lilburn and Alex Ciurak. © 2010 by Scholastic Inc. Permission granted to photocopy for nonprofit use in a classroom or similar place dedicated to face-to-face educational instruction.

Investigation 11

How far can you throw?

Choose three different types of balls and investigate which one you can throw the farthest.

Record your findings.

Things to consider

Where will you do the throwing?
Do you need someone to help you?
How will you measure the distances?
Do other students in your class have similar findings?

Investigation 12

Doubling numbers

I doubled the number 7 four times to reach a number above 100:

| 7 | 14 | 28 | 56 | 112 |

What other numbers have to be doubled four times to reach a number above 100?
What numbers have to be doubled more than four times?
What numbers have to be doubled four or less times?

Things to consider

Do you need a calculator to help you?
Can you see any patterns when doubling numbers?

Section IV

Tasks and Investigations, Grades 3–4

Tasks • Strand: Number

Money

Mom spent $45 at the supermarket. What might she have bought?	*You will need to provide supermarket advertisements and calculators. Note the students who round off amounts when using estimation. This task can be repeated on other occasions by varying the amount of money that is spent.*
I wrote three checks for different companies. The total amount of money was $785.60. How much might I have written on each check?	*Allow students to use calculators to check their answers.*

Fractions

A pizza was cut into ten equal size slices. Three people ate the whole pizza but each person had a different number of slices. Use fractions to describe the possible number of slices eaten by each of the three people (for example, $\frac{1}{10} + \frac{5}{10} + \frac{4}{10}$).	*Note any students who are able to use equivalent fractions to describe the slices (for example, $\frac{1}{10} + \frac{1}{2} + \frac{4}{10}$).*
If the shape shown here is one-fourth of a larger shape, what might the larger shape look like?	*This requires students to show a whole shape or area that is four times the area of the given shape. You might like to ask students to identify the given shape within their larger shape and ask them how they know it represents one-fourth.*
One-fourth of a bunch of balloons is red. Draw what the bunch of balloons might look like.	*This task requires students to show part of a group or collection. Are the parts shown equal? Can students give more than one answer?* See Rubric 4, page 12.

Tasks • Strand: Number

Decimals and Percentages

A student said that 4.25 was larger than 4.5 because there were three digits in 4.25 and only two in 4.5. Do you agree? If not, write some decimal numbers that are larger than 4.5.	*This task highlights a misconception that some students may have. Ask students to explain their answers.*
We are numbers that look like __.__ __ and we are between 7.0 and 9.0. One of our digits is 5. What numbers might we be?	*Check that students record their answers systematically.*

Numeration

The digits in a three-digit number between 300 and 500 add up to 9. What might the number be? Write all possible numbers.	*Do students record their answers systematically and know when they have recorded all possibilities?* See Rubric 5, page 14.
I am thinking of a number between 8,000 and 9,000. Its hundreds digit is 5 and its units digit is 2. What might the number be?	*Ask students to write all possible numbers. Note students who do this systematically so they know they have recorded all possible numbers.*
I halved a number and kept halving the new number a total of five times. The answer was a number between 1 and 10. What number might I have started with?	*Do students realize that they can start with a number between 1 and 10 and keep doubling five times to find an answer? Choose students to describe how they did this task.*
Look at the following sequence: 1, 7, 13, 19, 25. . . . Is 80 a member of this sequence? Explain your reasoning.	*Note the reasons students give for their answers. Can students make a decision without counting by sixes?*
A car license plate had the digits 3, 6, and 2, but I can't remember what order they were in. What might they have been?	*Do students record their answers systematically and know when they have recorded all possibilities?*

Tasks • Strand: Number

Operations

What combinations of three numbers on a hundreds grid (0 to 99) total more than 260?	*Allow students to use calculators to help them record combinations of numbers. Encourage students to use estimation too.*
When playing a game of bowling I got a score of 18. If there were ten pins, each with a different number from 1 to 10, what numbers might I have knocked down to receive a score of 18?	*Apart from 10 and 8, students need to record combinations of three different numbers that make 18.*
What might the missing numbers be? __ __ + __ = 63	*There are ten possible answers: 63 + 0, 62 + 1, 61 + 2, 60 + 3, 59 + 4, 58 + 5, 57 + 6, 56 + 7, 55 + 8, and 54 + 9.*
The difference between two three-digit numbers is 47. What might the two numbers be?	*Which students choose a three-digit number and add 47 to it to find two possible numbers? Ask students to find multiple solutions to this task.*
What might the missing numbers be? __ × __ = 50.	*Students should record all possibilities with whole numbers.*
Describe how you would subtract 19 from 83 in your head. What other subtractions could you do using a similar method?	*The most likely method students would use is to round 19 to 20, subtract 20 from 83 (63), and then add 1 back on (64). Other subtractions they might suggest include different examples where 19 is subtracted, examples where 9, 29, 39 . . . is subtracted, and examples where 11, 21, 31 . . . is subtracted.*
The number 17 cannot be divided equally by either 2 or 3. What other numbers are not divisible by either 2 or 3?	*Share the strategies students use to find numbers that are not divisible by either 2 or 3. You may prefer to ask students to write ten other numbers that are not divisible by either 2 or 3, or to write all numbers between two given numbers, for example, 1 and 100.* See Rubric 6, page 16.

continues

Tasks • Strand: Number

Operations, *continued*

Hannah wrote a sentence that had exactly sixty letters. What might her sentence be?	*This task involves lots of addition. Vary the task by asking students to write sentences containing other numbers of letters.*
A telephone number has eight digits that when added together make a total of 47. What might it be?	*Ask students to do this without a calculator. Share the strategies students use to find the totals. For example, do they look for pairs of digits that make ten, add doubles, start from the largest digit, and so on?*

Patterns and Algebra

Ben grouped the following numbers together: 21, 15, 45, 24, 6, and 30. What other numbers might belong in Ben's group?	*Do students realize that any number that is divisible by 3 can belong in this group? This task can be used for other groups of numbers, such as: numbers that are divisible by 5, numbers that are divisible by 7, odd numbers, and even numbers.*
How many different ways can you complete this equation? $4 \times 6 = \underline{} \times \underline{}$	*Note those students who record all ways: 1×24, 2×12, 3×8, 6×4, 8×3, 12×2, and 24×1. Which students understand that multiplication is commutative, in other words, that the answer is the same no matter what order the numbers are in?*
Make this number sentence true in as many ways as you can: $\underline{} \times \underline{} = \underline{} \times \underline{}$	*This is similar to the previous task but is more open. Changing the signs to addition, subtraction, or division will vary this task. You could also present a combination of signs, for example, $\underline{} \div \underline{} = \underline{} + \underline{}$.*
I am thinking of a number so that when I triple it and add 12, the answer is an even number below 80. What number might I be thinking of?	*Students should find that the number is any even number from 2 ($2 \times 3 + 12 = 18$) to 22 ($22 \times 3 + 12 = 78$). Adapt this format for other numbers.*

Tasks • Strand: Number

I am thinking of a number so that when I take a quarter of it and subtract 7, the answer is an odd number between 0 and 20. What number might I be thinking of?	*This is similar to the previous task. Note the methods students use—some will use trial and error and others will work backwards. An example of working backwards is: Choose an odd number between 0 and 20 such as 3, add 7 to make 10, then multiply 10 by 4 to make 40, so the number you are thinking of could be 40.*
Lauren used red and yellow blocks to build a tower that was six blocks tall. What might her tower look like?	*Provide blocks and drawing paper for this task. Note any students who do not realize that there is more than one possible tower. Which students develop a systematic way to record the possible towers? Share successful strategies. Asking students to use three colors can easily extend this task.*
Record a number sequence of at least eight numbers where each new number is five more than the previous number.	*Students can start their sequence at any number. Share the completed sequences. Vary this task by changing the rule that links successive numbers. For example: each new number is twenty fewer than the previous number; each new number is twice the previous number. Make the task more advanced by using fractions or decimals.*

Tasks • Strand: Measurement

Weight

Three animals have a combined weight of 253 pounds. One of the animals weighs 84 pounds. What might each of the other animals weigh?	*This task is about addition and subtraction as much as weight. Ensure students give realistic weights for their answers.*
Three objects in your classroom have a combined weight of about 4 pounds. What might the objects be?	*Students do not need to give exact weights for this task. Note those students who understand the relationship between ounces and pounds.*

Volume and Capacity

Mom bought four bottles that contain a total of 3.5 gallons of juice. How much juice might each bottle contain?	*Provide a range of juice containers for students to do this task. How easily can students convert between ounces, quarts, and gallons?*

Length and Perimeter

Kate drew a shape that had a perimeter of 15 inches. What might her shape have looked like?	*You will need to provide rulers and paper for this task. Some students might be able to record the dimensions on a sketch of their shape rather than constructing it. Do students realize that many shapes are possible?*
The entrance to a tunnel was 4.3 feet high. Who in your class would be able to enter the tunnel without bending?	*Provide measuring equipment for this task.*
I have drawn an irregular straight-sided shape with a perimeter of 7 inches. What might my shape look like?	*Students should mark the dimensions on each side of their shape. Share the shapes that students draw. Do all students understand what an irregular shape is?*
Find some things in the room that are between 1 foot and 1 yard in length.	*This task will indicate if students understand the relationship between feet and yards.*

Tasks • Strand: Measurement

The difference in height between you and another person is about 6 inches. Who might the other person be?	*Do students realize that the other person can be 6 inches taller or shorter?*

Area

A framing shop was making frames with different dimensions but all with an area of 24 square inches and selling them for the same price. What dimensions might the frames have?	*Possible whole number dimensions are 1 × 24, 2 × 12, 3 × 8, and 4 × 6 but students should realize that a frame that is either of the first two dimensions is unlikely to be useful.*

Time

What are some things you do between 11 a.m. and 2 p.m.?	*The purpose of this is to check that students understand a.m. and p.m.*
Kim said that he could walk to his house in five minutes. What are some places at school that you could walk to in one minute?	*Students will need timers and measuring equipment. This task also involves length, location, and position.*
I left home before noon and fifty minutes later arrived after 12 noon at my appointment. When might I have left home and when might I have arrived at my appointment?	*This task checks if students can calculate times before or after a certain time. Which students can give the full range of possible times?*
A boat took seven-and-a-half hours to travel between two islands. It left when it was dark and arrived when it was light. What might its departure and arrival times have been?	*Note if students are confident when doing time calculations. Ask students to use a.m. and p.m. when recording possible times.*

Tasks • Strand: Geometry

Location and Position

If you travel southeast from your school, name three places that you will come to.	*Change the direction to fit your situation. Do students understand that southeast is not just places in their immediate environment but can be places much farther away? You may want to provide maps for this task.*

Two-Dimensional Shape

A poster in our classroom had the heading *two-dimensional shapes with straight sides.* What shapes might have been on the poster?	*Ask students to draw some possible shapes. After students have drawn shapes, cut the shapes out and use them for classification activities.*
I used two squares to make one larger shape. What might my larger shape have looked like?	*You could use any combination of two or more shapes to do this task. For example, two rectangles, one square and one triangle, or three squares. Do students realize that the two squares do not have to be congruent?*
I drew a shape that contained four right angles. My shape was not a square or a rectangle. What shape might I have drawn?	*Provide paper so that students can draw possible shapes. Ask them to mark the right angles on each shape to check that there are four. Share the finished shapes so students see that there are many possibilities.*
An octagon was drawn so that none of its sides were parallel. What might it look like?	*Display the completed shapes. Check that all shapes are octagons and ask students to say how they know this. Ask students to say how they can check that no sides in each octagon are parallel. Choose students to demonstrate.*
I drew a shape that had two acute angles. What might my shape look like?	*A similar task could be done for shapes with no angles, no right angles, two obtuse angles, and so on.*
Kelly drew a picture of a house with exactly twenty-four right angles, six acute angles, and two obtuse angles. What might her house look like?	*Ask students to check each other's drawings by identifying and counting the specified angles.*

Tasks • Strand: Geometry

The shape shown below is one-fourth of a larger shape. Draw what the larger shape might look like.	*You can adapt this task by changing the shape and/or the fraction.*
Lucy drew a shape on the board and said that it was a rectangle. Draw what Lucy's shape might have looked like and then describe the features her shape must have to be called a rectangle.	*Share the shapes that students draw. Use the students' ideas to make a class list of the features of a rectangle.*

Three-Dimensional Shape

At least one of the faces of a prism is rectangular. What might the prism look like?	*Have a variety of three-dimensional shapes available for students to choose from. Make sure to include some shapes with a rectangular face that are not prisms (for example, a pyramid with a rectangular base). The purpose of this task is for students to understand the characteristics of a prism. Some students may like to attempt to draw suitable prisms. Does anyone know that the nets of many cylinders have a rectangular face?*
A three-dimensional shape was built by using tape to join five two-dimensional shapes together. What might the three-dimensional shape look like?	*Triangular prisms and square pyramids both have five faces. Students may like to cut out faces and join them together to make a three-dimensional shape with five faces.*
Some students used two triangular prisms and one rectangular prism to construct a model. What might their model have looked like?	*Have plenty of boxes, cardboard, and tape available. Students can either use boxes shaped like triangular and rectangular prisms or they can make their own out of cardboard and tape. Share the finished models so students can see the wide range of possibilities. Ask students to identify the three-dimensional solids in each model.*

Tasks • Strand: Probability and Data

Probability

Emily spun a spinner twenty times. It landed on red and yellow eight times each, on green three times, and on blue once. Draw a diagram to show what the spinner might look like.	*Allow students to make a spinner to match their diagram and try it out to see if the results are similar to the ones described.*
What are some outcomes that have a 1 in 2 chance?	*Can students offer a range of suitable responses? Possible responses include: choosing a red card from a deck of cards, tossing an even number on a standard dice, and a tossed coin landing on heads.*
At a family math night, people take a chance to draw a red ball from a bag of balls without looking. If they draw out a red ball, they win a prize. I watched ten people do this activity and only two of them won prizes. Draw what the balls in the bag might look like.	*There could be any number of colored balls in the bag but only a small number of them would be red. Based on the information given, if ten people had a turn and only two won, there could be ten balls in the bag, two of which are red. Students at this level often overestimate their chances of winning, so it is a good idea to make some of the bags suggested by students and allow them to have turns at drawing out a ball.*
Design a simple activity that could be played at a family math night, in which a player has the same chance of winning a prize as not winning a prize.	*Students could work in small groups to complete this task. Discuss if the activity would be a good one for a family math night. If you have time, do some of the activities designed by students and see how successful they are in having an equal chance.*

Data

Sketch a line graph to show how hungry you might be from the time you get out of bed until after you have eaten lunch.	*Share the completed graphs with the class and choose different students to identify the points on each graph where students were hungriest and where they were not hungry.*
A survey of pets owned by a class of students showed that there were more cats than dogs and more dogs than birds. What might the graph look like?	*This task allows students to interpret the data in their own way. Make sure that students use realistic numbers and look for any students who are able to display data using many-to-one correspondence.*

Investigation 1

Crazy counting

1	2	3	4	5	6	7	8	9	10
11	12	13	14	15	16	17	18	19	20
21	22	23	24	25	26	27	28	29	30
31	32	33	34	35	36	37	38	39	40
41	42	43	44	45	46	47	48	49	50

Investigate which number is most frequently said when counting to one hundred if one student starts counting in twos, another student in threes, another in fours, another in fives, and another in sixes.

What number do you think will be said the most? _____

Record all your counting here.

What did you find?

Was the number you predicted above the one that was said the most?

What other numbers are frequently said?

Are there any numbers that are never said? What do these numbers have in common?

Things to consider

Will a number chart help? If so, use the one on Reproducible 5.
How can you tell if a number will be in a counting pattern without counting?

Investigation 2

Apply the rule

Here is a pattern that mathematicians are trying to prove. That is, they want to be sure that the rule works in every case.

Begin with a number of your choice.

If your number is even, divide it in half.

If your number is odd, multiply it by 3, then add 1.

Whatever answer you get, apply the rule over again, then again, and again and again.

Example 1:

11

11	x	3	=	33
33	+	1	=	34
34	÷	2	=	17
17	x	3	=	51
51	+	1	=	52
52	÷	2	=	26
26	÷	2	=	13
13	x	3	=	39
39	+	1	=	40
40	÷	2	=	20
20	÷	2	=	10
10	÷	2	=	5
5	x	3	=	15
15	+	1	=	16
16	÷	2	=	8
8	÷	2	=	4
4	÷	2	=	2
2	÷	2	=	1

Example 2:

5

5	x	3	=	15
15	+	1	=	16
16	÷	2	=	8
8	÷	2	=	4
4	÷	2	=	2
2	÷	2	=	1

Do this with as many numbers as you can.

Describe any patterns that you find.

Things to consider

Does it work for all numbers be they one-digit, two-digit, or three-digit?
Will a calculator help?

Investigation 3

Top secret

Writing in code is fun, especially when numbers are substituted for letters.

Write some words that are worth exactly 500 if:

$$A = 26, B = 25, C = 24 \ldots Z = 1$$

Write your words here, showing the calculations you used for each word.

Design your own code using letters and numbers.

Things to consider

Are vowels more frequent in words than consonants?
Is there a way of estimating the value of words before undertaking a calculation?
Will a calculator help?

Investigation 4

Park your car

A company had a vacant block that measured 90 feet x 150 feet and decided to use it as a parking lot until a new building was constructed. If they allowed an area 9 feet x 18 feet for each car, how many cars could they fit on their parking lot?

Design your parking lot below.

Things to consider

Cars need space to be able to get in and out of a parking space.
There must be an entrance and exit.
Have you used all the space efficiently?

Investigation 5

Battery power

Do all brands of batteries last the same amount of time?

You will need different brands of new batteries. They should all be the same size and fit one of your toys.

Record your findings here.

Things to consider

How will you time how long a battery lasts?
Is it possible to test more than one brand of battery at the same time?
How will you record your findings?

Investigation 6

How big is one thousand?

Place value is the value a digit has because of its position in a number. The same digit can have different values depending on its position in a number.

4 346

value 4,000   value 40

Investigate where you would find 1,000 things.

Write what you have found out on a separate sheet of paper.

Do you think that 1,000 students would fit on your school playground?

Show how you worked it out.

Can you write 1,000 numbers on the board?

Show how you worked it out.

Things to consider

Will knowing the dimensions of a school playground or classroom board help?
Will an estimate be accurate enough?

From *Investigations, Tasks, and Rubrics to Teach and Assess Math* by Pat Lilburn and Alex Ciurak. © 2010 by Scholastic Inc. Permission granted to photocopy for nonprofit use in a classroom or similar place dedicated to face-to-face educational instruction.

Investigation 7

Doggone dilemma!

Many people won't buy a dog because they say it is too expensive to feed.

Investigate this claim by finding out how much it would cost to feed a dog over its lifetime.

Show your calculations here.

Things to consider

Do all dogs eat the same amount?
How long do dogs live?
What food do dogs eat?
How accurate does your estimate need to be?

Investigation 8

Flag design

The government of Terraman decided that the country needed a new flag. They surveyed the citizens of Terraman about preferred colors and discovered that $\frac{3}{8}$ preferred red, $\frac{1}{4}$ preferred blue, $\frac{1}{8}$ preferred green, and $\frac{1}{4}$ preferred yellow.

It was decided to incorporate all colors in this new flag with $\frac{3}{8}$ of the flag red, $\frac{1}{4}$ blue, $\frac{1}{8}$ green, and $\frac{1}{4}$ yellow.

Design a flag for Terraman that fits the above decision.

Investigate the flag designs of Panama and Hungary and work out what fraction of the flag each color is.

Things to consider

Would folding paper help?
Is there more than one possible design for this flag?

From *Investigations, Tasks, and Rubrics to Teach and Assess Math* by Pat Lilburn and Alex Ciurak. © 2010 by Scholastic Inc. Permission granted to photocopy for nonprofit use in a classroom or similar place dedicated to face-to-face educational instruction.

Investigation **9**

Reading backwards

Palindromic numbers read the same both forward and backward.

For example, 87, 978, and 13,431 are the same forward and backward.

Write some palindromic numbers of your own in the space below.

Investigate numbers that are not palindromic.

Write a number that is not a palindrome: For example:　　　　123 Reverse it:　　　　　321 Add the two numbers:　444 (123 + 321) Now you have reached a palindrome.	Note: Sometimes it will take a few more steps before a palindrome is reached. For example:　　　　　　317 Reverse it:　　　　　　　713 Add the two numbers:　1030　(317 + 713) Reverse it:　　　　　　　0301 Add the two numbers:　1331 (1030 + 301) Now you have reached a palindrome.

Investigate the number of steps it takes to reach a palindrome for the numbers on this chart.

Number	Number of Steps	Palindrome
68		
241		
472		
553		
943		

How many numbers from the chart turned into palindromes after one reversal? How many needed more than one reversal? Did any not turn into palindromes?

Things to consider

Will you need a calculator?
Do you need paper?

Investigation 10

Money bags

Maria took a bag of coins to the bank. When the coins were placed on the scales they weighed 1 pound. If all the coins were the same value:

How many coins were there?

What was their total value?

Write how you worked it out and what you discovered.

From *Investigations, Tasks, and Rubrics to Teach and Assess Math* by Pat Lilburn and Alex Ciurak. © 2010 by Scholastic Inc. Permission granted to photocopy for nonprofit use in a classroom or similar place dedicated to face-to-face educational instruction.

Things to consider

Is there more than one possible solution?
Will you need to collect a pound of each type of coin to work this out?
Do you think a pound of 5-cent coins would have a greater value than a pound of 10-cent coins?

Investigation 11

Length units

In Papua New Guinea, many people do not use standard units, such as the metric system, to measure length. They use familiar objects, such as hand and arm spans, string, bamboo, and rope to measure length.

A *span* is defined as the distance from the tip of the little finger to the thumb when the fingers are spread.

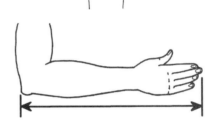

Builders in ancient Egypt used a measure called a *cubit*.

The cubit was defined as the distance from the elbow to the outstretched middle finger.

Several other body parts were used to measure, for example:
a palm: the width across the four fingers of a hand
a hand: the distance across all four fingers and thumb

Measure five members of your class to determine their span and cubit. Present the measurements in a table.

Design your own nonstandard unit of measurement and use it to measure some lengths in your classroom. Write about what you found.

Things to consider

Do you know of any other nonstandard measurement units that are used to measure lengths? Why do we use standard units?

Investigation 12

Common names

Jessica's name begins with J and two of her friends have names that begin with J (Josie and Jana).

What letter seems to be the most common with which to begin a first name?

Things to consider

How many names of people will you need to collect?
Do you think the most common letter is the same for girls' and boys' names?
Does the most common letter change depending on the age group of the people you survey?

From *Investigations, Tasks, and Rubrics to Teach and Assess Math* by Pat Lilburn and Alex Ciurak. © 2010 by Scholastic Inc. Permission granted to photocopy for nonprofit use in a classroom or similar place dedicated to face-to-face educational instruction.

Investigation 13

Stamp arrays

Stamps can be purchased in rectangular sheets of varying size and number. Investigate how many different ways sixty stamps could be organized onto one sheet for sale.

Things to consider

What strategy will you use to solve this?
How will you know when you have found all the different ways?

Add four numbers

Mrs. Tamblyn told her students interesting information about some numbers. She said that the smallest number that can be made by adding four numbers fewer than 10 is 4 (1 + 1 + 1 + 1) and the largest number that can be made in the same way is 36 (9 + 9 + 9 + 9).

Investigate ways that the other numbers (5 to 35) can be made by adding four numbers fewer than 10 together. *Example: One way to make 7 is 2 + 1 + 1 + 3.*

Things to consider

Is there only one way to make each number?
How will you know when you have found all possibilities for a number?

From *Investigations, Tasks, and Rubrics to Teach and Assess Math* by Pat Lilburn and Alex Ciurak. © 2010 by Scholastic Inc. Permission granted to photocopy for nonprofit use in a classroom or similar place dedicated to face-to-face educational instruction.

Investigation 15

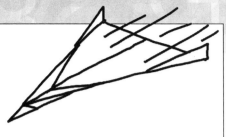

Plane launch

Design your own paper plane using a blank sheet of paper. Launch your plane, time the duration of its flight, and measure the distance it flew. Repeat the launch three times and record your measurements in a table.

Modify your plane and describe the modifications that you made here.

Launch your modified plane three times and record your measurements in another table.

Write what you have found on a separate sheet of paper.

Things to consider

How will you measure duration?
How will you measure length?
Will you need another student to help you?
Will wing shape and area affect the flight of your plane?

Investigation 16

Deliver the mail

Mailboxes can come in a variety of shapes and sizes. A school decided to ask students to design a new mailbox that would accommodate all incoming mail the school received each day.

Design a new school mailbox. Draw it below and mark all dimensions.

Things to consider

How can you find out how much mail is received each day?
What type of incoming mail will the mailbox receive each day?
Is more mail received on certain days?

From *Investigations, Tasks, and Rubrics to Teach and Assess Math* by Pat Lilburn and Alex Ciurak. © 2010 by Scholastic Inc. Permission granted to photocopy for nonprofit use in a classroom or similar place dedicated to face-to-face educational instruction.

Investigation 17

Well read!

How many books would you need to make a stack that would reach the ceiling of your classroom?

Record your estimate here: _____

With a few classmates, discuss how you can check your estimate.
Decide on a strategy and carry it out.

In the space below, write about how you checked your estimate and what you found.

Things to consider

Do you need to make a stack to the ceiling to work this out?
Is there more than one possible answer?
Are all the books the same thickness?

Investigation 18

High flyer

My mom read this puzzle in an airline magazine:

Choose a digit from 1 to 9.
Multiply 37,037 by the digit you chose.
Multiply the result by 3.

For example:
Choose the digit 5.
Multiply 37,037 by 5. (37,037 x 5 = 185,185)
Multiply the result by 3. (185,185 x 3 = 555,555)

Mom decided to investigate what would happen if she chose a digit other than 5 and was surprised by what she found. By the time she had finished her investigation the airline had almost arrived at its destination.

Investigate what happens when you follow the process described above with the other digits from 1 to 9.

Show your calculations below.

What have you found?

Things to consider

Will a calculator be useful?

From *Investigations, Tasks, and Rubrics to Teach and Assess Math* by Pat Lilburn and Alex Ciurak. © 2010 by Scholastic Inc. Permission granted to photocopy for nonprofit use in a classroom or similar place dedicated to face-to-face educational instruction.

Investigation 19

Home sweet home

If a lion requires an enclosure with an area of 30 yd², what shape could this enclosure be?

Draw your enclosure here, including measurements.

Things to consider

What type of features must be included in a lion's enclosure?
Will square-inch paper (see Reproducible 10) help you draw the enclosure?

Investigation 20

Right or left?

Do all right-handed people kick with their right-foot and all left-handed people kick with their left foot?

Do you agree? _____

Work out a way to prove your answer. Record your method and results below.

Things to consider

How many people will you need to sample?
How will you record your data?

Investigation 21

Traffic lights

How much time should traffic lights allow for people to cross the road?

Use the space below to record your findings and recommendations.

Things to consider

Are all crossings the same width?
At what speed does the average person walk?
How will you measure the time?

Investigation 22

Lengthy names

I looked at a list of all student names in my class and noticed that most of the students' last names were between five and eight letters in length.

Does this apply to the students in your class?

Things to consider

Will a class list of names help?
Will a table help you to organize last names into categories?

Investigation 23

Towering students

Which pairs of students in your class have a total height of 8.8 feet?

Use this space to record your calculations.
Don't forget to record the name and height of each student in a pair.

Things to consider

Will grouping students in your class by height help?
Are there different combinations of students that will make this height?

Investigation 24

Will it be white?

What is the chance that the next car to pass your school will be white?

Record your method and findings here.

From *Investigations, Tasks, and Rubrics to Teach and Assess Math* by Pat Lilburn and Alex Ciurak. © 2010 by Scholastic Inc. Permission granted to photocopy for nonprofit use in a classroom or similar place dedicated to face-to-face educational instruction.

Things to consider

How many cars will you have to survey?
Where on the school grounds will you stand so that you can easily see passing cars?
What will you use to describe your findings? Words, numbers. . .?

Tasks and Investigations, Grades 5–6

Tasks • Strand: Number

Money

A group of students spent $120 at the supermarket when shopping for their class picnic. If they bought everything that was needed for the twenty-six students in their class, what might they have bought?	*You will need to provide students with supermarket advertisements and calculators. As a class decide if students have to find goods to the value of $120 exactly or if you will accept $5 either side of this. Check if students use estimation skills to help them. Note how they use the calculator. When students have finished their shopping lists, compare and discuss the merits of each. Ask various students or groups of students to justify the items and quantities they have on their lists.*
The marketing manager of a travel company was confident that his company would book overseas tours to the value of about 800,000 dollars. What value of tours might the company actually book?	*Are students aware that the number of dollars can be above and below 800,000? Ask students to give more than one response or to provide a range. If they can give the entire range (750,000 to 849,000) it shows they have a complete understanding of the rounding concept.*

Fractions

The number of students at one school was $\frac{2}{3}$ the number of students at another school. What number of students might have been at each school?	*Students will need to look for numbers that are multiples of 3, for example, 120 students at one school and 80 students at another school. Observe how students do this task.*
Sharmin wrote fractions that were smaller than $\frac{1}{4}$. What fractions might she have written?	*Do students write fractions that have numerators other than one? Some students may think a fraction with a denominator smaller than 4 will be smaller than $\frac{1}{4}$.* See Rubric 9, page 22.
Amber said that $\frac{3}{4}$ was equivalent to $\frac{30}{40}$. What other fractions are equivalent to $\frac{3}{4}$?	*Ask students to say how they know which fractions are equivalent to $\frac{3}{4}$. You can use any fraction you like for this task.*

continues

Tasks • Strand: Number

Fractions, *continued*

Alex solved a story problem and wrote the answer of $\frac{3}{5}$. What might the story problem have been?	*It is important to share the completed story problems so students can see the variety of possible responses.*
Two fractions are added together to make $\frac{2}{5}$. Other than $\frac{1}{5} + \frac{1}{5}$, what might the two fractions be?	*The purpose of this task is for students to understand that denominators other than 5 are possible. For example, $\frac{2}{10} + \frac{2}{10}$, $\frac{1}{10} + \frac{3}{10}$, and $\frac{1}{15} + \frac{5}{15}$ all equal $\frac{2}{5}$.*
Draw a situation to match the ratio 3:9. Explain how your drawing matches the ratio.	*Do students realize that they do not have to draw 12 items? A ratio of 3:9 can be simplified to 1:3 so a drawing that shows, for example, 1 tent for every 3 students would be suitable.*
India and Jess have been given a bag of individually wrapped chocolates. If India takes $\frac{1}{4}$ of the chocolates and Jess takes $\frac{1}{5}$, how many chocolates might have been in the bag and how many might still be in the bag?	*Do students understand that the number of chocolates in the bag initially must be a number that has 4 and 5 as factors (20, 40, 60 . . .)? Do students use this to calculate the number of chocolates that each girl takes and the number that are left in the bag?*
$\frac{\triangle}{\triangle} \times$ ___ $= 8$ What might the missing numbers be?	*The missing numbers do not have to be the same as each other. Two possible answers are $\frac{1}{2} \times 16 = 8$ and $\frac{1}{3} \times 24 = 8$. Can students find all the possibilities? (There are eight possible answers.)*
Some pancakes were shared among a number of people. Each person got $2\frac{1}{5}$ pancakes and there were none left over. How many pancakes might have been made and how many people might have shared them?	*Do students realize that the number of people has to be a multiple of five so that the number of pancakes is a whole number? If they multiply $2\frac{1}{5}$ by 5 (people) they will get 11 (pancakes), $2\frac{1}{5}$ by 10 (people) they will get 22 (pancakes), $2\frac{1}{5}$ by 15 (people) they will get 33 (pancakes), and so on.*

Tasks • Strand: Number

Holly spent exactly $\frac{1}{8}$ of the money she had saved on a present for her sister, exactly $\frac{1}{4}$ of it on a present for her brother, and exactly $\frac{1}{3}$ of it on a present for her parents. How much money might Holly have spent on each present and how much might she have saved?	Do students realize that the total amount of money must be a multiple of 8, 4, and 3, such as $24, $48, or $72? Once they have established this then they can calculate the amount spent on each present.
Kim converted a fraction to 60 percent. What might the fraction have been?	Ask students to give at least five answers. Possible answers include: $\frac{3}{5}$, $\frac{60}{100}$, $\frac{6}{10}$, $\frac{9}{15}$, and $\frac{30}{50}$.
A fraction is simplified to $\frac{1}{4}$. What might the fraction be?	The purpose of this task is to see if students understand equivalence of fractions and have strategies to create equivalent fractions. Ask students to give more than one equivalent fraction.

Decimals and Percentages

I am thinking of a number that has a 9 in the tenths place. What might my number be?	Note students who use the decimal point correctly. Who records numbers with hundredths also (for example, 5.96, 475.98, 32.911)?
The difference between two decimal numbers is 8.56. What might the two numbers be?	Ask students to give more than one answer. Note the methods students use to do this. Who records a decimal number and then adds 8.56 to it?
Nick multiplied 4.8 by 3.3 and got an answer of 158.4. What did he do wrong? What could he do in future to make sure he doesn't make the same mistake?	This task has to do with the placement of the decimal point. Students need to understand that if they estimate the answer by rounding (5 × 3 = 15) then they will always place the decimal point in the correct position.

continues

Tasks • Strand: Number

Decimals and Percentages, *continued*

Tessa said the answer to 37.6 × 6 was 2,256 and the answer to 28.4 × 7 was 1,988. What is she doing wrong? What advice could you give her to help her get the correct answers?	*This, like the previous task, has to do with the placement of the decimal point. Students need to understand that the decimal point separates whole numbers from parts of numbers.*
In a long-jump competition Sarah jumped 2.4 meters and Jessica jumped 2.04 meters. Sarah came first and Jessica came third. What distance might the girl who came second have jumped? What distance might the girl who came fourth have jumped?	*The main purpose is to check that students can order decimals.*
__.__ × 5 = __.__ What might the missing numbers be? Try to find all possibilities.	*Do students know that whole numbers can be recorded as decimals? (for example, 0.2 × 5 = 1.0)? Can they record all possibilities systematically from 0.1 × 5 = 0.5 to 1.9 × 5 = 9.5?*
I calculated a percent of a number and got the answer 10. What percent and what number might I have used in my calculation?	*Possible answers for this include 100 percent of 10, 50 percent of 20, 10 percent of 100, and 25 percent of 40.*
In a swimming event the times are measured to hundredths of a second. The winner's time was 38.52 seconds. What might be the times of the other seven swimmers?	*The emphasis here is on ordering decimals. Note how realistic the times are. You could discuss if a time like 39.2 is possible when times are measured in hundredths to see if students understand that 39.2 is the same as 39.20.*
Write different sets of numbers to fit these number sentences: __.__ × __.__ > 65 and __.__ × __.__ < 20.	*Allow students to use calculators to check their responses. Which students use estimation to help them choose suitable numbers?*
The answer to a calculation was 17.8. What might the calculation have been?	*Encourage students to use the four operations. Allow them to use a calculator if they wish. Note students who record a broad range of calculations including those like: 178 ÷ 10, 1780 ÷ 100, 1.78 × 10, and so on. Repeat this task with different decimals.*

Tasks • Strand: Number

A set of four decimal numbers has a median of 3.5. What might the four numbers be?	*This task has links with decimals and data. Students need to understand that the median of a set of numbers where the number of numbers is even is found by calculating the average of the two middle numbers when the numbers are placed in order.*

Numeration

The number 25,617 can be written as 20,000 + 5,000 + 600 + 10 + 7. What are some other ways it can be written?	*Students should be able to give a variety of answers. Note if students are confident when moving between ten thousands, one thousands, one hundreds, tens, and ones.*
A chart of the decimal numbers from 5.01 to 6 was cut up to make a jigsaw. The numbers 5.25 and 5.43 are on the same jigsaw piece. What might the rest of the piece look like?	*It is a good idea to supply students with a hundreds grid so they can enter the decimal numbers and then use the grid to work out a possible jigsaw piece. You could specify the number of squares on the jigsaw piece if you want, for example, five squares. Share the students' work so everyone can see the range of possible answers.*
Will thinks that 23 and 33 are prime numbers because they end in 3, which is a prime number. Matt says Will is wrong. Who is correct and why?	*This task highlights a misconception that some students may have.*
Write some different numbers that when rounded to the nearest tenth give 21.3.	*The numbers can include or be more than 21.25 but must be fewer than 21.35. Those students who can give the entire range of possible numbers have a better understanding of the concept of rounding than students who can only give one or two numbers.*

continues

Grade
5–6

Numeration, *continued*

Find four consecutive odd numbers with a sum between 160 and 200.	*Ensure that students understand the term* consecutive *and that they find more than one group of four numbers. They could do the same for four consecutive even numbers and for five consecutive odd or even numbers.*
Draw various number lines that each have at least six numbers marked at equal intervals and include the number 180,000.	*Make sure students understand that their number line can start from any number and end on any number (for example, 165,000, 170,000, 175,000, 180,000, 185,000, 190,000 or 180,300, 180,200, 180,100, 180,000, 179,900, 179,800.) Note those students who write numbers in descending order, do not use equal intervals, or who do not include any intervals. Share the completed number lines and allow students to work out what each is counting by.* See Rubric 7, page 18.
The difference between the highest and lowest temperature on a certain day was 10°F. The lowest temperature was below zero. What might the two temperatures have been?	*This task will indicate if students are comfortable when dealing with negative numbers.*

Operations

If 17 fish are divided equally between 3 bowls, how many will be in each bowl and how many will be left over? The answer to this division story is 5 remainder 2. Write another division story where the answer is 5 remainder 2.	*Note the methods students use to work out the numbers that will give an answer of 5 remainder 2. Share the completed stories and check that they do give the stated answer.*
The answer to a division number sentence is between 20 and 30. What might the division number sentence be?	*Do students use multiplication to help them find suitable division number sentences?*

Tasks • Strand: Number

I multiplied two numbers together and got an answer of 2,300. What are the possibilities?	*Encourage students to be systematic in their thinking. Which students do this by division and which do it by trial and error multiplication? Who uses doubling and halving? For example, if 10 × 230 = 2,300, then 20 × 115 and 5 × 460 will also equal 2,300. A similar related task might be: I multiplied three numbers together and the product was 2,400. What might the three numbers have been?*
Amy shared 64 cards equally between herself and a friend so that they each got 32. How many other ways can 64 be shared equally among friends (without a remainder)?	*Students should record all possibilities.*
When I tossed two eight-sided dice and multiplied the results, I got a product that was an odd number. What numbers might have been on the dice?	*Students should record all possibilities. Note those who develop a system for recording.*
38 × 12 and 327 – 259 both have answers that are even. Write other calculations that you know will have an even answer.	*Encourage students to record calculations using each of the operation signs. You could also ask them to record calculations that have an odd answer. Ask students to say how they know if an answer will be even or odd before they work it out.*
Three schools raised a total of $125,750 for charity. Each school raised a different amount but were within $3,000 of each other. What amount might each school have raised?	*The total can be varied to suit the students you have in your class. To make the task easier, omit the part about being within $3,000 of each other. A similar task can be stated as: __ + __ + __ = 125,750*
Three hundred and forty-four sheep were put into pens with the same number in each pen. What number of pens might there be and how many sheep in each?	*Note the methods students use to do this. Do they use multiplication to check their division?*

continues

Operations, *continued*

If the 8 key on your calculator is missing how could you calculate 144 × 8?	*Three possible ways students could do this are: multiply by 7 and then add on 144; multiply by 4 and double the answer; multiply by 9 and subtract 144. Share the ways they suggest.*
A whole number is multiplied by five. Write some numbers that could result from this multiplication.	*Note how students work out calculations. Do they choose numbers and multiply them by five to find the results or do they know that any whole number multiplied by five will end in zero or five and choose numbers accordingly?*
Find some three-, four-, or five-digit numbers that will make this number sentence true: __ − __ = __	*Record students' responses on the board so that they can see that there are many possible solutions.*
A number of students could make groups of four or groups of six without having any students left over. How many students might there be?	*Do students realize that it can be any number that has both 4 and 6 as factors?*

Patterns and Algebra

Danni wrote a number. It was larger than 1,000 but smaller than 10,000 and did not contain any even digits. Its digits added up to 16. What number might she have written?	*Note students who do this methodically. Which students realize that any combination of the digits 1, 3, 5, and 7 will produce a total of 16? Students can also use the same digit twice in a number (for example, 9115, 9133 or 5533).*
Make this number sentence true in as many ways as you can: __ ÷ 4 − 5 = __.	*Explain to students that the symbols in this case can represent one-, two-, or three-digit numbers (for example, 96 ÷ 4 − 5 = 19 and 120 ÷ 4 − 5 = 25). Can any students use negative numbers (for example, 8 ÷ 4 − 5 = −3)?*

Tasks • Strand: Number

Finn wrote some equations that had an answer of 20. He only used one subtraction sign, one division sign, and one set of parentheses in each equation. What might his equations look like?	*Check that students understand the order of operations and have used parentheses appropriately. They should not use parentheses around division since division is done before subtraction anyway. Possible equations are 60 ÷ (12 – 9) = 20 and (100 – 20) ÷ 4 = 20.* See Rubric 8, page 20.
I worked out an equation and got the answer 30. I know there were two sets of parentheses, a division sign, and an addition sign, but I cannot remember any of the other signs or the numbers. What might the equation be?	*This is similar to the previous task but allows students to use signs other than those specified.*
Record a number sentence using all four operations. The answer should be 100. Only use parentheses where necessary.	*This is similar to the two previous tasks. The emphasis is on students using the correct order of operations and understanding where to use parentheses.*
Harry entered the following numbers into a function machine: 10, 16, and 22. The output numbers for these were 19, 31, and 43, respectively. Write other numbers that Harry might enter and record the matching output numbers.	*The main point of this is to see if students can find the rule that links two sets of numbers. In this case it is "double and subtract 1," but the task can be done for other rules too.*
Find solutions to this equation: $\triangle \diamond + \diamond \triangle = \square \square$	*Explain to students that each symbol represents a single digit, so that two two-digit numbers whose digits are reversed are added together to make another two-digit number whose digits are the same. For example, 12 + 21 = 33, 13 + 31 = 44, and 23 + 32 = 55 are three of the sixteen possible solutions. Encourage students to find all solutions. Note students who do this systematically.*

continues

Tasks • Strand: Number

Patterns and Algebra, *continued*

Write some numbers greater than 1,000 that have 2, 3, and 5 as common factors.	*Note those students who understand that when numbers share a factor it is called a common factor. Also note the methods students use to find numbers that are divisible by 2, 3, and 5.*
$16 \times 8 >$ ____ $+$ ____ What might the missing numbers be?	*Note students who understand that the missing numbers can be any two numbers whose total is not more than 127. You can vary this task by changing the > sign to <, or by changing the numbers and operations signs.*
Connor wrote a number and described it by saying that it was both odd and a square number between 100 and 500. What might the number be?	*The purpose of this task is to check if students are able to identify square numbers.*
When Darcy added two prime numbers together his answer was between 100 and 110. What numbers might he have added together?	*Can students identify prime numbers? Can they systematically work out pairs that have a total between 100 and 110? This task could be adapted by altering the range or by using square or triangular (for example, 3, 6, 10, 15, 21, 28, 36, 45, 55, 66, and so on) numbers.*
The rule connecting two sets of numbers is $B = A \times 6$. Draw a table of values, like the one shown here, and insert numbers to show this relationship.	*Vary this task by giving students different one-step rules such as $B = A \div 2$, $B = A - 10$, $B = A + 7$, and two-step rules such as $B = A \times 2 - 5$ and $B = A \div 2 + 10$.*

Set A					
Set B					

Tasks • Strand: Measurement

Weight

Dad bought a total of 3.85 pounds of fruit. He had five different types of fruit, all of which had different weights. What fruits might he have bought and how much might each type weigh?	*Are the weights that students relate to each fruit type realistic? Check how easily students can convert between ounces and pounds.*
The total weight of three kittens is $\frac{15}{16}$ lb. One kitten weighs $\frac{1}{4}$ lb. What could be the weight of the other two kittens?	*This task could also be under fractions as it involves an understanding of equivalent fractions. Can students work with fractions of a pound? You could ask students to give the weight of each kitten in ounces.*

Volume and Capacity

A prism was made with four layers each of nine cubes. What other ways can you make a prism with the same volume as that one?	*Do students understand how to calculate the volume of the described prism and can they use that to make other prisms of the same volume? You could ask students to draw their prisms.*
A school has a bake sale to raise funds. How many different ways could we pack twelve brownies, all the same size, to fit into a box?	*Students should record their answers by drawing and by recording the number of brownies that fit along the length, width, and height of a box.*
A container has a volume of 1 million cubic units but it is not shaped like a cube. What might its dimensions be?	*Students need to understand the dimensions can be any three numbers that multiply together to equal 1,000,000 (for example, 10 × 100 × 1000 or 200 × 100 × 50).*
An object made from cubic units has a volume of 7 cubic units. Draw what it might look like.	*You might like to provide centimeter-squared grid paper, one-inch grid paper, or isometric paper (see Reproducibles 9, 10, and 12). If students want, allow them to use cubes to construct objects before they draw them. Do students realize that objects made from 7 cubic units have a volume of 7 cubic units even when their faces are not aligned rather than being joined exactly?*

continues

Tasks • Strand: Measurement

Volume and Capacity, *continued*

A rectangular prism has a volume of 36 cubic units and one of its dimensions is 3. What might the other dimensions be?	*This task requires students to know that volume is calculated by the formula length × width × height. The three dimensions need to have a product of 36; because we are told one of the products is 3, the other two must be factors of 12: 1 and 12, 2 and 6, or 3 and 4.*
An object is made from two cubes, each with dimensions in whole units, joined together. It has a volume of fewer than 60 cubic units. What might its volume be?	*Do students realize that the two cubes do not have to have the same volume? Objects can be combinations of cubes of the following volumes: 1, 8, and 27 cubic units.*

Length and Perimeter

Ben fenced his garden with a particular type of fencing that cost $8.25 per yard. He spent $396 on the fencing and completely enclosed his garden. What might a plan of Ben's garden look like?	*Students have to first calculate the perimeter of the fence by dividing 396 by 8.25 (48) and then draw a plan of a garden that has a perimeter of 48 yards.*
Create a symmetrical design with a perimeter of 8 inches.	*This task also relates to two-dimensional shapes. You could also use other perimeter measurements such as 14 inches. To extend this task, ask students to investigate if it is possible to create a symmetrical design with a perimeter that is odd (for example, 11 inches).*
Rosie wrote a sentence that was about 10 inches long. What might the sentence have been?	*Provide rulers and lined paper for this task. Encourage students to write more than one sentence. Share the finished sentences so students realize that size and spacing of handwriting and the writing tool used can affect the outcome. You could also do this on a computer so that all students use the same font, size, and spacing. Note how students work out the length of their sentences. Which students measure out 10 inches and then try to fit a sentence in the space? Which students use their normal writing and adjust the words in their sentence until it is 10 inches long?*

Tasks • Strand: Measurement

Area

A shape made from two rectangles has an area of 16 square inches. What might this shape look like?	*Ask students to give at least five different responses and to mark the dimensions on each shape.*
Design some flower beds for a garden that cover exactly 14 square yards and are not rectangular in shape.	*Provide one-inch grid paper (see Reproducible 10) and discuss how a scale of 1 in = 1 yard can be used. As students are working note how they count the squares. Which students design flower beds using part squares?*

Time

Use a map to design a car trip that will take $1\frac{1}{2}$ hours travelling at an average speed of 70 mph. Show your planned journey.	*Students will need a map with a scale and a ruler. Share the planned journeys.*
We are traveling by car to a place that is 360 miles away. How long might it take us to get there? At what average speed per hour would we be traveling?	*Are students' responses reasonable? Do they allow for slowing down through towns and cities?*

Tasks • Strand: Geometry

Location and Position

Jamie used the scale 1 in = 1 yd to draw a diagram of a shape. Use the same scale to draw a shape that has a perimeter of 15 yards.	*Share the completed shapes so students can see that many different shapes are possible.*
Use a road map of the U.S. or your state to work out some places that are about 150 miles apart.	*Students need a map with a scale marked on it and a ruler. It is best to use a map of your state that has many places marked.*
Choose a page from a road map or atlas. List pairs of features that are about 0.5 miles apart.	*Are students able to use a ruler correctly?*
The network shown here is traversable. That is, it is possible to draw over it without retracing any line and without lifting your pen from the shape. Draw a network of your own that is traversable. 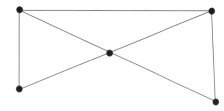	*Share the completed networks so students can check that they are traversable. A network is traversable only if an odd number of lines meet at fewer than three junctions.*
Terry calculated that the distance between two places on opposite sides of a map was about 1,000 miles. What might the map scale be?	*Look for realistic responses and ask students to justify them. For example, a scale of 1 in = 100 mi is only acceptable if the map is about 10 inches wide. A better response would be 1 in = 50 mi for a map that is 20 inches wide. If the map is very large then a scale of 1 in = 10 mi could be acceptable. Note those students who understand this.*

Tasks • Strand: Geometry

Two-Dimensional Shape

I drew a parallelogram on a grid like the one shown below. I recorded the coordinates for my parallelogram. What coordinates might I have written?

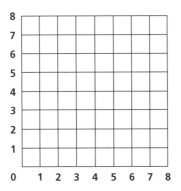

This task can be used for a variety of two-dimensional shapes.

Peter wrote some three-digit numbers and then realized that they had both vertical and horizontal symmetry. What numbers might he have written?

The only digits that could have both vertical and horizontal symmetry are 0, 1 and 8, so the three-digit numbers must contain combinations of those digits—for example, 888, 101, or 810. Students at this level could be asked to find all possible three-digit numbers.

Sweet Pea gave these instructions to her friend to help her find her way around Treat Town.
- Marshmallow St., Rocky Rd., and Caramel Ave. are all parallel.
- Licorice Lane is perpendicular to Marshmallow St. and ends at Caramel Ave.
- Candy Rd. is diagonal to Caramel Ave. and ends at Rocky Rd.
- Peanut Brittle Court runs off Licorice Lane.

What might a map of Treat Town look like?

This task checks if students understand the meaning of different linear terms. A secondary focus is on the different maps that match this description.

continues

Tasks • Strand: Geometry

Two-Dimensional Shape, *continued*

A shape has at least one pair of opposite angles that are congruent. Draw what the shape might look like.	*You may like to provide protractors for this task. Share the finished shapes. Use them for classification activities, such as shapes with one pair of opposite angles that are congruent and shapes with two pairs.*
If one angle in a triangle is 45 degrees, what might each of the other angles be?	*Do students know that the angles in a triangle total 180 degrees? Students may like to use a protractor to draw possible triangles. You could extend this task by asking students to draw both isosceles and scalene triangles. Discuss if it is possible to draw an equilateral triangle with an angle of 45 degrees.*
The angles in a shape add up to 360 degrees. What might the shape look like and how many degrees might each of its angles be?	*Do students realize that their shape must be a quadrilateral? They can use protractors to measure the angles in their shape and check that the total is 360 degrees.*

Three-Dimensional Shape

Six cubes were joined together, dipped in blue paint and then taken apart. Draw ways the cubes might have been put together so that when they were taken apart at least twenty-four faces were painted blue.	*You may like to supply centimeter-squared grid paper (see Reproducible 9) on which students can draw their cube designs. The designs below show three ways the six cubes might be joined together.* 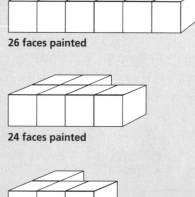 **26 faces painted** 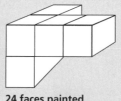 **24 faces painted** **24 faces painted**

Tasks • Strand: Geometry

The shape shown below is one-third of a larger shape. Draw what the larger shape might look like. 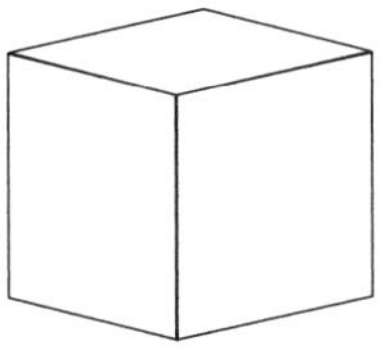	*This task is similar to a task in Two-Dimensional Shape on page 59 but is more suitable for grades 5 and 6 students as it is quite difficult to draw three-dimensional shapes. You may want to supply students with isometric paper (see Reproducible 12). You can adapt this task by changing the shape and/or the fraction.*
A three-dimensional object is made from four congruent cubes. What might a net of the object look like?	*Provide cubes and one-inch grid paper (see Reproducible 10). Encourage students to make four-cube objects before drawing their nets and to draw nets for more than one four-cube object. Note the methods students use to help them draw the nets. Some students might like to cut out their nets to check that they fold into the required object.*
Justin picked up a solid that was not a prism, pyramid, cylinder, or cone. What solid might he have picked up?	*The obvious answer is a sphere but it could also be an irregularly shaped solid or an octahedron, icosahedron, or dodecahedron. Ask students to justify why the shape they choose is not a prism, pyramid, cylinder, or cone.*

Tasks • Strand: Probability and Data

Chance

An event has a probability of 75 percent. What might the event be?	*One example is drawing a blue counter from a box that contains three blue counters and one red counter.*
Design a spinner that fits all these requirements: • All sections are equal. • A number is written in each section. • The probability of the arrow landing on an even number is $\frac{1}{3}$. • The probability of the arrow landing on a number above 40 is 50 percent.	*The smallest number of sections possible is 6 (lowest common multiple of 3 and 2) but students could have a spinner with 12, 18, or 24 sections. Share the completed designs and check that they satisfy the requirements.*
The probability that a certain card will be dealt from a shuffled deck of cards is $\frac{1}{13}$. What might the card be?	*Ask students to name all possible cards. It could be an ace, a queen, a king, a jack, or one of the number cards 2 to 10.*
Jill said that it was more likely that an ace would be dealt from a standard deck of cards than a red 3. Is she correct and, if so, what are some other cards that are more likely to be dealt than a red 3?	*The probability of an ace being dealt is $\frac{4}{52}$ ($\frac{1}{13}$). The probability of a red 3 being dealt is $\frac{2}{52}$ ($\frac{1}{26}$). Any card that has a better probability than $\frac{2}{52}$ is more likely to be dealt than a red 3.*
Design a dice where the chance of throwing a number greater than 10 is 50 percent.	*Share the completed designs. Students could either draw their dice or use a net for a cube if they are designing a six-sided dice. Do any students design dice with more than six sides?*
Design a set of number cards where the probability of choosing numbers is as follows: • A number with zero on the end is 25 percent. • A number above 100 is 75 percent. • An odd number is 50 percent.	*This is quite a challenging task. The smallest set of cards possible is four (for example, 110, 105, 106, and 97). However, students could have any number of cards in their set as long as it is a multiple of four.*

Tasks • Strand: Probability and Data

Data

The mean of a set of numbers is 8. There are seven numbers and each one is different. What might the numbers be?	*How do students use the mean to work out the numbers? Do they use the total of 56 or do they balance the numbers around 8 so that a number of 5 (8 – 3) would be balanced by a number of 11 (8 + 3)?*
The mean and the median of a set of nine numbers is 12. What might the numbers be?	*Do students understand the meaning of each term? Do they use the mean to calculate the total of the nine numbers?*
The mean of five decimal numbers is 6.7 and this is the second lowest of the five numbers. What might the other four numbers be?	*One possible answer is 3.2, 6.7, 6.8, 7.1, and 9.7. How do students use the total of 33.5 to work out possible numbers?*
Create three data sets each with six numbers. The first set should have 5 as the mode, the second set should have two modes, and the third set should not have a mode.	*The purpose of this task is to check that students understand the term mode. Share students' suggestions so they can see the range of possible sets.*
Seven people went fishing. The median number of fish caught was 4, the mean was 5, and the mode was 3. How many fish might each person have caught?	*Do students understand the meaning of each term? Share the responses so students see there is more than one possible answer.*
From eleven scores on a ten-point quiz, the mean is 8, the median is 8, and the mode is 7. What might the scores be?	*One possible solution is 4, 7, 7, 7, 7, 8, 9, 9, 10, 10, 10.*
What might this Venn diagram be about?	*Ask students to write a few sentences to describe the diagram. Also, ask them to label each circle. Share students' responses so they can see the variety of possible scenarios.*

Clever numbers

Follow the process below with at least ten more three-digit numbers in which two of the digits are repeated. Try this without using a calculator!

1. *Write down a three-digit number in which two of the digits are repeated (for example, 464).*

2. *Write down all the possible two-digit combinations of the three digits you used and add them together: 46 + 64 + 44 = 154.*

3. *Add the digits of the original number: 464 = 4 + 6 + 4 = 14.*

4. *Now divide the sum of the three-digit number (154) by the sum of the original number (14): 154 ÷ 14 = 11.*

What do you find?

Try this with three-digit numbers where the digits are all different, such as 417. What do you find?

What will happen if you try this same process with four-digit numbers, where two of the digits are repeated?

Things to consider

You may need some blank sheets of paper.

Investigation 2

Create a crossword

Crosswords are fun to complete but much more fun to create.

Create a crossword on centimeter-squared grid paper (see Reproducible 9) using addition, subtraction, multiplication, and division clues. When completed give it to a friend to solve.

Note: you must use each of the above processes at least three times in your crossword.

Things to consider

How will you decide on the size of your crossword grid?
How are you going to present clues and answers?
How will you check if your crossword is correct?
Fractions, decimals, and parentheses can be used to make your crossword even more challenging.

Investigation 3

Alphabet symmetry

Symmetrical shapes are pleasing to look at because they appear balanced. There are examples of symmetry all around us. Symmetry can be seen in the natural world—for example, butterfly wings, leaves, and shells—as well as objects we create and construct in two- and three-dimensions, such as buildings.

Symmetry can also be found in letters and words, for example, the word -BED-, where we see a horizontal line of symmetry.

Investigate the upper case letters of the alphabet for symmetry.
How many upper case letters have:

- vertical symmetry
- horizontal symmetry
- both vertical and horizontal symmetry
- rotational symmetry?

Write some words that are symmetrical.
Can you write a symmetrical sentence?

Things to consider

There are different types of symmetry.

Mirror symmetry (also known as bilateral, reflection or line symmetry): When a shape is folded vertically or horizontally and its two halves match.

Rotational symmetry: Where the shape looks the same when turned around a central point less than a full turn (for example, an equilateral triangle).

From *Investigations, Tasks, and Rubrics to Teach and Assess Math* by Pat Lilburn and Alex Ciurak. © 2010 by Scholastic Inc. Permission granted to photocopy for nonprofit use in a classroom or similar place dedicated to face-to-face educational instruction.

Investigation 4

Stepping out!

Medical experts have recommended that everyone walk at least 10,000 steps a day to stay healthy.

How far do you walk in a day? Do you meet the 10,000 steps/day guideline?

How far do you walk in a week, a month, a year?

Things to consider

When do you walk at school? Moving around the school, lunchtime activities, and so on?
How will you measure walking activities?
What walking do you do outside of school hours?
Can you count exercise other than walking as part of the 10,000 steps? If so, how will you measure it?

Investigation 5

Divide by three

If the digits in a number are added together and the total is divisible by 3, then the number is also divisible by 3.

For example, the digits in 3,528 total 18 (3 + 5 + 2 + 8) and 18 divided by 3 is 6, so 3,528 is divisible by 3 (3,528 ÷ 3 = 1,176).

Investigate if this is true for all numbers.

Things to consider

You may like to use a calculator to help you with this investigation.
You may like to choose a range of numbers to investigate (for example, numbers from 500 to 600).

Investigation 6

Traffic jam!

During peak hour traffic on a three-lane freeway, a truck braked suddenly and rolled over, causing chaos. Within a short time, all vehicles on a three-mile stretch of the freeway came to a halt.

How many vehicles might have been caught in this traffic jam?

Things to consider

What types of vehicles might be traveling on the freeway?
How long are vehicles and how much space is there between vehicles?

Investigation 7

Smart packaging

Companies continually redesign their product packaging to make it stand out and be more appealing than their competitors' products.

Design and construct a package for a new product soon to be released in supermarkets.

Present the package as the product with its own label.

Prepare a promotional brochure to support your product.

Use this space for your initial design ideas.

Things to consider

The type of product will determine the type of packaging required.
What material will you use? Plastic, cardboard . . .?
What will be the best shape for your product? Cylindrical, rectangular . . .?
What information will you include on the label?

Investigation 8

Anyone for tennis?

The four grand slam tennis events—The French Open, Wimbledon, The U.S. Open and The Australian Open—all run as knockout tournaments. The draw pairs tennis players and the winner of each pair stays in the tournament until they are beaten.

The physical education teacher at Springwood School is planning a knockout tennis tournament for sixty-four students. She needs to work out the total number of matches to be played so that teachers know when students need to be released from class.

- Draw the physical education teacher's tournament plan.

- How many matches will be played in total?

- List the possible numbers of players that can compete in a knockout competition.

- Can you make a knockout tournament for twenty-four players?

Things to consider

Look at professional knockout tournaments and see how they are structured.
Why do tournament organizers use byes?

Investigation 9

Four 4s

I have been told that it is possible to make all the numbers between 1 and 100 by using four 4s and any operation. For example: $4 \div 4 + 4 - 4 = 1$.

Make as many of the numbers between 1 and 100 in this way to see if it is possible.

Things to consider

Use the four processes in a variety of ways.
Are parentheses useful in some situations?

From *Investigations, Tasks, and Rubrics to Teach and Assess Math* by Pat Lilburn and Alex Ciurak. © 2010 by Scholastic Inc. Permission granted to photocopy for nonprofit use in a classroom or similar place dedicated to face-to-face educational instruction.

Investigation 10

Clock design

Many countries use the metric system for measurement. The units in this system are all related by multiples of ten. For example, there are 100 cm in a meter, 1,000 grams in a kilogram, and so on.

Time is one measurement that is not metric. Our system of measuring time seems to have come from the ancient Sumerians who used a counting system based on 60, hence 60 seconds in a minute and 60 minutes in an hour.

Design a "metric" system for measuring time.

Things to consider

Milliseconds (hundredths of a second) are already in existence, and these are based on the powers of ten. Can you use this as a starting point?

Did you know that in China's recorded history there were two systems of time? The day was divided both into one hundred parts and into twelve double hours. The Jesuits introduced Western time into China during the seventeenth century.

Investigation 11

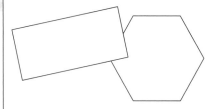

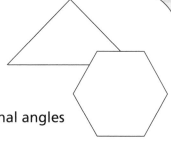

Angles in shapes

A triangle is a polygon with three straight sides. The sum of the internal angles of any triangle is 180 degrees.

A quadrilateral is a polygon with four straight sides. The sum of the internal angles of any quadrilateral is 360 degrees.

Investigate the internal angles of regular and irregular pentagons to see if all pentagons have the same angle sum.

Do the same for regular and irregular hexagons.

Write a report to show what you have found.

Things to consider

How will you measure the angles?
How many shapes will you need to review before you can write your report?

From *Investigations, Tasks, and Rubrics to Teach and Assess Math* by Pat Lilburn and Alex Ciurak. © 2010 by Scholastic Inc. Permission granted to photocopy for nonprofit use in a classroom or similar place dedicated to face-to-face educational instruction.

Investigation **12**

Sample me!

The Mars Company produced the following data showing the frequency of colors in a package of M&M's.

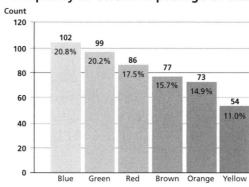

Frequency of Color in a package of M&M's

Plan a class investigation to check the above data. Collect your data on a separate sheet of paper. Record your data as a graph here.

How similar/different are your findings compared to the figures given above?

What do you think would happen if you did this activity again?

Things to consider

What sampling methods will you use?
What can you do to get a larger sample?

Ratio

The Golden Ratio is a ratio of length to width and is approximately 1:1.618. This ratio not only appears in art and architecture, but also can be observed in nature and in the human body.

The Golden Ratio is the ratio of a person's total height to height from their feet to their navel.

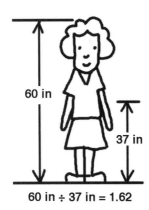

60 in

37 in

60 in ÷ 37 in = 1.62

How does your total height compare to the height from your feet to your navel? Is it close to the Golden Ratio?

Investigate other lengths, such as the distance from the waist to the floor and from the top of the head to the waist, to see whether a similar ratio exists between those measurements. Enter your data on a chart.

How does your data compare to other members of your class?

Things to consider

How will you compare your data with other students in your class?

Investigation 14

Good Luck!

Good-luck letters

Max wanted to send a good-luck message. He didn't want to write too many letters, so he decided to write a good-luck message to five of his friends and ask them in turn to write to five of their friends who would then write to five of their friends.

How many letters were written altogether?

Show your thinking here. (If you need more space, continue on another sheet of paper.)

Investigate how many letters would be written if Max sent this letter to six friends.
Investigate how many letters would be written if Max sent this letter to ten friends.

Things to consider

How are you going to solve this problem?
What strategy will you use to help you solve this problem?
Do you think there is more than one way to solve this problem?

Tired digits

Tim's teacher was discussing the number 1,000,000 and challenged her students to write down all the numbers from 1 to 1,000,000. Tim thought that it would be an easy thing to do but after writing 28,905 digits his hand ached and he was tired of the challenge.

- What number did Tim get up to?

- How many digits are there altogether in the numbers 1 to 1,000,000?

- If Tim wrote one digit each second, how long would it take him to write all the numbers up to 1,000,000?

Things to consider

What is the difference between a digit and a number?
Can you organize numbers according to their number of digits?
Would a numbered chart with the numbers 1 through 100 (see Reproducible 5) be useful?
Will you need a calculator?

From *Investigations, Tasks, and Rubrics to Teach and Assess Math* by Pat Lilburn and Alex Ciurak. © 2010 by Scholastic Inc. Permission granted to photocopy for nonprofit use in a classroom or similar place dedicated to face-to-face educational instruction.

Investigation 16

Dispose of plastic

Plastics are the most common litter item found on Earth Day roadside clean-ups. Plastics persist in the environment for hundreds of years. Many countries produce one million tons or more of plastic every year.

How much plastic does your school dispose of in a year?

How much is this per person in your school?

Things to consider

What products are made of plastic?
How will you measure the amount of plastic your school uses?
How exact does your calculation have to be? Will an estimate be enough?

Magical hats

You have been asked by a magician to act as his assistant during performances. Before you can start, you have to make a hat that fits you and that is sturdy and large enough to be used for performing magic tricks.

Draw a design below for a magician's hat to fit you. Include all relevant measurements.

Draw a net of your design on flexible cardboard and then cut it out and join it together to make your hat. Sketch the net in this space.

From *Investigations, Tasks, and Rubrics to Teach and Assess Math* by Pat Lilburn and Alex Ciurak. © 2010 by Scholastic Inc. Permission granted to photocopy for nonprofit use in a classroom or similar place dedicated to face-to-face educational instruction.

Things to consider

How will you work out the circumference of your hat so that it fits on your head?
How will you strengthen your hat so that it can be used for tricks?

Investigation *18*

Front-page news

The first page of a newspaper generally includes the title, all the publication information, the index, and the main stories that will capture the most attention. The major story of the day is placed in the most prominent position and has a large, boldfaced headline.

A survey in 2001 summarized a newspaper's front-page content over seven days as the following:

Categories	Circulation		
	50–100,000	100–200,000	200,000+
stories that continue onto next page	63.1%	76.7%	76%
average number of photos per story	0.8%	1.0%	1.0%
local news focus	47.1%	44.7%	42.6%
national news focus	30.4%	31.4%	26.8%
international focus	6.5%	8.3%	12.4%

Find three newspapers each with a similar circulation to those listed above.

Investigate the above categories with each paper. How similar/different are your findings compared to the figures given above?

Things to consider

Can you share newspapers with other students so you don't have to collect information from three papers each day for seven days?

How will you record your daily findings?

How will you find the average over seven days?

Would using a news website instead of newspapers be more appropriate for you?

How will you divide up the tasks? Will you use estimation?

Investigation 19

Reach and height

Reach (also known as wingspan) is the physical measurement of the length from one end of an individual's arms (measured at the fingertips) to the other when raised parallel to the ground at shoulder height. The average **reach** correlates to the person's **height**.

Did you know that an above-average reach is advantageous in sports such as basketball and boxing? For instance, the boxer Sonny Liston had an 83.9-inch reach despite being 71.7 inches in height. This unusually long reach allowed him to hit opposing boxers from relatively safe distances where they could not reach him.

Who in your class has the greatest difference between their reach and their height?

Does the tallest student have the greatest total reach?
Does the student with the longest arms have the greatest reach?

Things to consider

How will you measure reach and height?
How will you present your findings so that they are easy to interpret?

From *Investigations, Tasks, and Rubrics to Teach and Assess Math* by Pat Lilburn and Alex Ciurak. © 2010 by Scholastic Inc. Permission granted to photocopy for nonprofit use in a classroom or similar place dedicated to face-to-face educational instruction.

Investigation 20

Puzzling tangrams

A seven-piece tangram is a square puzzle made up of five triangles of various sizes, a square and a parallelogram. Tangram pieces can be used to make new shapes.

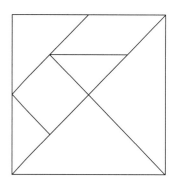

Cut out the pieces of the tangram on Reproducible 11 and use them for the investigations below.

Investigate how to make a square, a triangle, a rectangle, a trapezoid, and a parallelogram using all seven tangram pieces for each shape. Draw your shapes below.

Try to make seven squares of any size using first one tangram piece, then two pieces, then three, four, five, six, and seven pieces. Is this possible? Draw your shapes below.

Things to consider

Will rotating and flipping tangram pieces help to make shapes?
Is there more than one way to make some of the shapes?

Investigation 21

Drink and count

Soft drinks come in a variety of flavors and container sizes and advertising often targets teenagers.

How many soft drinks does the average teenager drink in a year?

Write your prediction here _____

Work out a way to check your prediction and do it.

How accurate was your prediction?

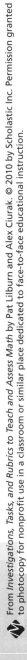

Things to consider

How will you define a teenager?

What strategy will you use to help you solve this problem?

How exact does your calculation have to be? Will an estimate be enough?
How will you justify your estimate?

Do you think there is more than one way to solve this problem?

Investigation 22

Take a shortcut

The answer to 53 x 11 can be found by adding the 5 and 3 together to make 8 and then placing the 8 between the 5 and 3 to make 583 (53 x 11 = 583).

The answer to 68 x 11 can be found by adding the 6 and 8 together to make 14 and then placing the 4 between the 6 and 8 and adding the 1 to the 6 to make 748 (68 x 11 = 748).

Can all numbers between 10 and 99 be multiplied by 11 in this way?

Things to consider

Can you explain why when the total of two digits is more than nine you cannot put that total between the two digits like you can when the total is nine or fewer than nine?

Investigation 23

Stretch your writing!

If you straightened out each of the lines in all your handwriting, how long a line would you write in a day?

Write your prediction here _____

Work out a way to check your prediction.

How accurate was your prediction?

Things to consider

How much writing do you do each day?
Will sampling a few of your handwritten words help?
What measurement tools might help you?

Investigation 24

Feel the pulse

To take your pulse, place one or two fingers on the back of your wrist on the thumb side, until you feel your pulse. Count the number of beats over a ten second period and multiply your count by six to find how many times your heart beats in one minute.

What is the average pulse rate of students in your class:

- when resting
- when exercising
- one minute after exercise
- two minutes after exercise
- five minutes after exercise?

Record your findings in a table.

Summarize your findings as a written report on another sheet of paper.

Things to consider

How will you collect data from students in the class?
Would it be useful to allocate sections of this investigation to various students?
How will you work out an average?
What will you use to ensure your timing is accurate?

Section VI
Additional Reproducibles

My Investigation Summary

Before the investigation

What do I have to do?

_____

_____

_____

What materials do I need?

_____

_____

_____

How am I going to do it?

_____

_____

_____

_____

_____

After the investigation

What did I do?

_____

_____

_____

What did I find out?

_____

_____

_____

_____

Would I use the same approach again? Why or why not?

_____

_____

_____

Rubric template 1

Write students, names in the circles according to the criteria for each category. This rubric is useful where students don't clearly belong in one of the three major categories.

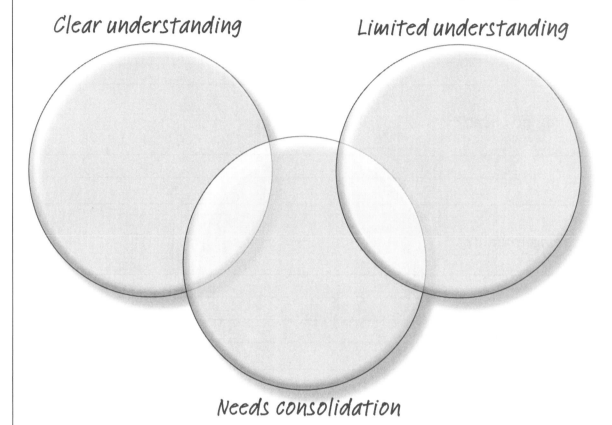

Clear understanding   Limited understanding

Needs consolidation

Task: _____

_____

Criteria

Clear understanding	Needs consolidation	Limited understanding

Rubric template 2

Task: _____

_____

Rating	Category	Criteria	Students
4	Goes beyond expectations.		
3	Demonstrates clear understanding.		
2	Acceptable but incomplete.		
1	Made an attempt but shows limited understanding.		
0	No understanding evident.		

Rubric template 3

Task: _____

_____

Rating	Category	Criteria	Students
5	Goes beyond.		
4	Task accomplished. Central mathematical ideas clearly demonstrated and understood.		
3	Substantial progress toward completing the task.		
2	Attempts task and makes some progress. Partial but limited grasp of the central mathematical ideas.		
1	Little progress or understanding evident.		

1–100 number chart

1	2	3	4	5	6	7	8	9	10
11	12	13	14	15	16	17	18	19	20
21	22	23	24	25	26	27	28	29	30
31	32	33	34	35	36	37	38	39	40
41	42	43	44	45	46	47	48	49	50
51	52	53	54	55	56	57	58	59	60
61	62	63	64	65	66	67	68	69	70
71	72	73	74	75	76	77	78	79	80
81	82	83	84	85	86	87	88	89	90
91	92	93	94	95	96	97	98	99	100

101–200 number chart

101	102	103	104	105	106	107	108	109	110
111	112	113	114	115	116	117	118	119	120
121	122	123	124	125	126	127	128	129	130
131	132	133	134	135	136	137	138	139	140
141	142	143	144	145	146	147	148	149	150
151	152	153	154	155	156	157	158	159	160
161	162	163	164	165	166	167	168	169	170
171	172	173	174	175	176	177	178	179	180
181	182	183	184	185	186	187	188	189	190
191	192	193	194	195	196	197	198	199	200

1-200 number chart

1	2	3	4	5	6	7	8	9	10
11	12	13	14	15	16	17	18	19	20
21	22	23	24	25	26	27	28	29	30
31	32	33	34	35	36	37	38	39	40
41	42	43	44	45	46	47	48	49	50
51	52	53	54	55	56	57	58	59	60
61	62	63	64	65	66	67	68	69	70
71	72	73	74	75	76	77	78	79	80
81	82	83	84	85	86	87	88	89	90
91	92	93	94	95	96	97	98	99	100
101	102	103	104	105	106	107	108	109	110
111	112	113	114	115	116	117	118	119	120
121	122	123	124	125	126	127	128	129	130
131	132	133	134	135	136	137	138	139	140
141	142	143	144	145	146	147	148	149	150
151	152	153	154	155	156	157	158	159	160
161	162	163	164	165	166	167	168	169	170
171	172	173	174	175	176	177	178	179	180
181	182	183	184	185	186	187	188	189	190
191	192	193	194	195	196	197	198	199	200

One-inch grid paper

Seven-piece tangrams

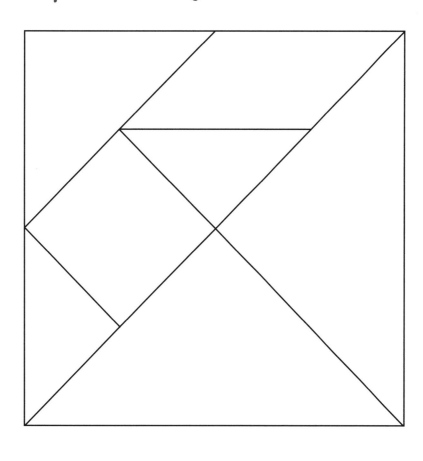

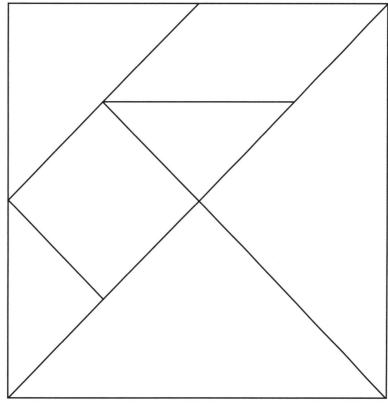

Isometric paper